SLAUGHTER ON
NORTH LASALLE

SLAUGHTER ON NORTH LASALLE

ROBERT L. SNOW

BERKLEY BOOKS, NEW YORK

THE BERKLEY PUBLISHING GROUP
Published by the Penguin Group
Penguin Group (USA) Inc.
375 Hudson Street, New York, New York 10014, USA
Penguin Group (Canada), 90 Eglinton Avenue East, Suite 700, Toronto, Ontario M4P 2Y3, Canada
(a division of Pearson Penguin Canada Inc.) • Penguin Books Ltd., 80 Strand, London WC2R 0RL,
England • Penguin Group Ireland, 25 St. Stephen's Green, Dublin 2, Ireland (a division of Penguin
Books Ltd.) • Penguin Group (Australia), 250 Camberwell Road, Camberwell, Victoria 3124, Australia
(a division of Pearson Australia Group Pty. Ltd.) • Penguin Books India Pvt. Ltd., 11 Community
Centre, Panchsheel Park, New Delhi—110 017, India • Penguin Group (NZ), 67 Apollo Drive,
Rosedale, Auckland 0632, New Zealand (a division of Pearson New Zealand Ltd.) • Penguin Books
(South Africa) (Pty.) Ltd., 24 Sturdee Avenue, Rosebank, Johannesburg 2196, South Africa

Penguin Books Ltd., Registered Offices: 80 Strand, London WC2R 0RL, England

The publisher does not have any control over and does not assume any
responsibility for author or third-party websites or their content.

SLAUGHTER ON NORTH LASALLE

A Berkley Book / published by arrangement with the author

PUBLISHING HISTORY
Berkley premium edition / July 2012

ISBN: 978-0-425-25047-1

BERKLEY®
Berkley Books are published by The Berkley Publishing Group,
a division of Penguin Group (USA) Inc.,
375 Hudson Street, New York, New York 10014.
BERKLEY® is a registered trademark of Penguin Group (USA) Inc.
The "B" design is a trademark of Penguin Group (USA) Inc.

PRINTED IN THE UNITED STATES OF AMERICA

10   9   8   7   6   5   4   3   2   1

Most Berkley Books are available at special quantity discounts for bulk purchases
for sales, promotions, premiums, fund-raising, or educational use. Special books,
or book excerpts, can also be created to fit specific needs.

For details, write: Special Markets, The Berkley Publishing Group,
375 Hudson Street, New York, New York 10014.

To Craig, Melinda, and Corbin
and to
Cindy, Dan, and Skylah

PERSONS INVOLVED IN THE
NORTH LASALLE STREET CASE

Victims

Robert Gierse—age 34, co-owner of B&B Microfilming
   Service Company, shared house with Robert Hinson
Robert Hinson—age 27, co-owner of B&B Microfilming
   Service Company, shared house with Robert Gierse
James Barker—age 27, best friend to Hinson and Gierse

Police Investigators

ORIGINAL INVESTIGATING OFFICERS:
Lieutenant Joseph McAtee
Sergeant Michael Popcheff
Sergeant James Strode
Sergeant Pat Stark
Sergeant Robert Tirmenstein

OFFICERS INVOLVED IN THE 1990s:
Detective Jon Layton
Lieutenant Louis Christ
Lieutenant Charles Briley

OFFICERS INVOLVED IN THE 2000s:

Sergeant Roy West

Deputy Deborah Borchelt

Select Other Notable Persons

Mary Cavanaugh—supposed witness to crime

Floyd Chastain—former coworker of Carroll Horton's

James T. Cole—Louise Cole's husband

Louise Cole—secretary at B&B Microfilming Service Company

Ilene Combest—Robert Gierse's ex-girlfriend

Ted Gierse—brother of victim Robert Gierse

Fred Harbison—employee of Ted Uland's in his oil business

Carroll Horton—Diane Horton's ex-husband

Diane Horton—Robert Gierse's girlfriend at the time of his death

John Karnes—friend of the three victims and discoverer of the crime

David Lynn—April Lynn Smoot's husband

Aleene Marcum—Robert Hinson's girlfriend at the time of his death

Angel Palma—Fred Harbison's daughter

Carol Schultz—investigative reporter

April Lynn Smoot—Robert Gierse's ex-girlfriend

Ted Uland—Gierse and Hinson's former employer at Records Security Corporation

Edward Dean Watson—insurance agent

Wava Winslow—James Barker's girlfriend at the time of his death

PART ONE
1971

CHAPTER ONE

"I just scored number twenty-five!"

James Barker couldn't keep from grinning as he bragged to his friend Robert Hinson about his latest sexual conquest. The woman had just gotten dressed and left minutes ago. Barker had watched through the blinds until she had driven away and then ran back to the telephone. He needed to take a shower, but that could wait. What couldn't wait was calling Bob Hinson and rubbing it in. It was nearing the end of 1971, and twenty-seven-year-old Barker knew that neither Hinson nor his other close friend Robert Gierse stood much chance of catching him. He was going to win! Gierse had only scored with twenty women so far that year, while Hinson, because he had uncharacteristically become emotionally involved and dated the same woman for almost an entire month, had scored with only eighteen.

In just a little over a month, on December 31, there would no longer be any doubt about which of the three friends was the most successful with the ladies. Barker knew that he couldn't gloat forever about his victory, but he still planned to savor it for a while. And if he knew his two friends, they would undoubtedly demand a rematch in 1972.

At the beginning of 1971, Gierse, Hinson, and Barker had entered into a friendly competition with one another. None of them were one-woman type of guys. They all liked to date around. And so, as might be expected, they'd had conversations and friendly arguments about who was the smoothest with the ladies, each man declaring *he* was. They finally decided to put it to the test. They would see who, by the end of 1971, could have sex with the most women. But to make it more difficult, one of the rules for the competition was that, in order to count, none of the women could have slept with either of the other two men. This meant that the women in 1971 would have to be mostly new, as the three men had often dated and shared the same women.

So far, by the end of November 1971, the total stood at sixty-three women, with Barker in the lead at twenty-five. The loser of the competition, the three men had agreed, would have to treat the others to an expensive dinner at a fine restaurant. It would be a great meal for the winner, who could not only gloat, but also make the loser pay to hear about it. To keep a running total of their sexual conquests, the three men maintained a scorecard at the North LaSalle Street house where Gierse and Hinson lived. At the end of each month the men would record in an address book the names of the women they had slept with. No real proof was required. The three men all knew one another well enough to trust the others not to cheat.

The three bachelors, all good-looking and smooth-talking, were known around Indianapolis in 1971 as men who worked hard and played hard. At thirty-four, Bob Gierse was the oldest of the group; both Bob Hinson and Jim Barker were twenty-seven. The three of them were the best of friends and hung out together constantly. They didn't believe in doing anything halfway. They always threw themselves totally into their work, but they also knew how to really enjoy themselves in their off time.

Several years earlier, all three men had been employed by the Bell and Howell Company in Chicago. Among other things, Bell and Howell manufactured microfilm equipment and supplies, which is the department the three men had worked in. Barker now worked as a service manager for the Bell and Howell plant in Indianapolis, having moved to the city a few years earlier, following his former coworkers Gierse and Hinson. They told him they had wanted to look for new business opportunities, but Barker liked the security of having a job with a company he could depend on. Gierse and Hinson had already changed jobs three times, working for two different microfilm companies over the previous couple of years.

By November 1971, Gierse and Hinson had just started their own already extraordinarily successful microfilm company called B&B (for Bob & Bob) Microfilming Service Company, located only a little over a mile from the modest white bungalow they shared on North LaSalle Street.

Barker lived alone in a small house at 1535 North Rural Street on the east side of Indianapolis, about a half mile from Gierse and Hinson's house at 1318 North LaSalle Street. Neither house would ever be part of a home tour, but for three single men, the houses fit their purposes.

When first coming to Indianapolis, Gierse and Hinson had rented, but in 1970 Gierse had taken over a $9,200 mortgage for the two-bedroom home on North LaSalle. And while the small house sat in the midst of a quiet middle-class neighborhood on the east side of Indianapolis, where the residents had always enjoyed tranquil, peaceful evenings, neighbors would later tell the police that ever since the two men had moved into the house there had been a constant party going on. Young women were always coming and going, but never quietly, it seemed. The music at the house, the neighbors complained, blared day and night, and the liquor apparently never stopped flowing.

The competition to win the contest became so intense that near the end of 1971, according to the *Indianapolis Star* newspaper, a neighbor of Barker's warned him, "Jim, you're not going to live long. You can't stand the pace." But during 1971, neither Barker nor the other two men worried about their health or even considered slowing down. Each one had believed when they started the contest that he would be the winner.

Yet still, even though their contest demanded constant womanizing, the three men, when establishing the rules for the competition, also reportedly made it a part of the agreement to never set up dates for Friday nights. That was the night the three of them would prowl cheap bars, the kind of places where the ceilings always had water stains and the vinyl seat cushions were always torn.

Going to lowbrow taverns had been a part of their friendship from the start. It was a bonding experience that they all enjoyed. But a big part of the reason for doing this, it would later be found, was the ego boost they got out of it. They could go to these bars and feel superior to everyone else there. Also, and very importantly, these bars were great for picking up the type of women they liked, though seldom without a bit of confrontation with the other men who hung out there. None of the three men cared if the woman he was trying to pick up was there with another man. A shoving match or actual fistfight wasn't uncommon, or even unwelcome. All three of the men knew how to fight and frankly enjoyed it when someone challenged them.

On the last Friday of November 1971, Hinson had gotten into a fistfight with the boyfriend of a go-go dancer at the Hi Neighbor Tavern on West 10th Street in Indianapolis, the scuffle breaking out after Hinson had reportedly patted the dancer on her buttocks. Hinson, at six feet two and weighing 255 pounds, knew how to use his fists and had pummeled the boyfriend.

Other than on Friday nights, however, there was a steady stream of young women in and out of the North LaSalle Street house throughout all of 1971, and also in and out of Barker's house on North Rural Street, several blocks west. Neighbors would later tell the police that the women came and went at all hours, and seldom was it the same women. A young lady who began dating Hinson near the first of November 1971, later interviewed by the police, said that she never saw Barker or Gierse with the same woman twice. She also said they almost always had a drink in their hand. Hinson reportedly told the young lady when they started dating, "Don't get involved. This is all for fun." And, she found, he meant it.

This contest among the three men, however, also had a serious side—throughout 1971, there began to be a number of ugly scenes at both North LaSalle and Barker's house involving angry, jilted women. This would include yelling and screaming, and also cars squealing their tires as they left. A friend of the three men recounted a visit to the house on North LaSalle Street during the last of November 1971—upon stepping inside, he found two very angry young women making a loud scene in the living room, while in the bathroom a third, semi-nude, woman scrubbed Gierse's back as he sat in the tub, apparently oblivious to what was going on in the other room.

None of this, though, slowed the three men in their

desire to beat the other two. Throughout the year, each man had put forth his best effort in order to be the winner.

On December 1, 1971, however, the contest ended abruptly, with no winner.

A business acquaintance and friend of Gierse and Hinson, twenty-nine-year-old John Karnes—who would later become an Indianapolis police officer—called the offices of B&B Microfilming Service on the morning of December 1, 1971, and asked for Gierse or Hinson. He needed to talk to them about a business matter. The secretary at B&B, Louise Cole, told Karnes that the two men had mentioned to her as she was leaving the previous afternoon that they planned to work very late that night, and so they hadn't come in yet. They were likely, she said, sleeping in. Karnes said she was probably right. He knew how hard Gierse and Hinson were working to make their new company a success. He told Cole he would try again later.

But when Karnes checked back in later that afternoon, Mrs. Cole said she still hadn't heard from either man and that she was becoming a bit concerned. While she knew well how both men loved to party, she also knew that Gierse and Hinson were extremely hardworking and dedicated to their new company. This just wasn't like them. Karnes reassured her that they were probably fine, and then told her that he would drive by the North LaSalle Street address and check on them.

Karnes arrived in the 1300 block of North LaSalle Street at about 2:15 P.M. on Wednesday, December 1, 1971. He found both Bob Hinson's black Oldsmobile 442 and Bob Gierse's blue Cadillac Coupe de Ville parked on the street in front of their house. This wasn't unusual, as they always parked on the street since they kept their garage packed with files waiting to be microfilmed. But strangely, Karnes also noticed, Jim Barker's blue Mustang sat there, too. That *was* unusual. Barker should have been at work.

Karnes parked his own car and then walked around to the rear of the house to see if perhaps the men were working on some files in the unattached garage. That could explain why they hadn't answered the telephone. Maybe Barker had taken the day off to help them; Karnes knew that Gierse and Hinson had been trying to get Barker to quit Bell and Howell and come join them in their new company.

It was a chilly December day, with the temperature in the midthirties. There had been some light freezing drizzle and snow flurries earlier, but Karnes knew that the weather wouldn't stop the men from working in the garage. Very little would stop them.

However, when he didn't see anything in the backyard other than two lawn chairs and a red charcoal grill, and no one in the garage, Karnes walked back around front and up onto the porch of the house. A low electric charge raced through his stomach when he saw the morning newspaper still on the porch and found mail in the mailbox. Something wasn't right. No matter how hard they partied or worked, he'd never known his friends to sleep in this late.

"Bob?" Karnes called, pulling open the screen door and knocking. "Bob, are you there?" When no one answered, he tried the front door and found it unlocked. That worried him because the people in the neighborhood didn't leave their doors unlocked. Now even more anxious, he called out again before finally pushing open the front door of the quiet, darkened house, the odor of stale beer instantly assailing his nostrils. "Is anyone here?"

When Karnes stepped into the living room and saw the twenty or so empty Stroh's beer bottles scattered around, and spied a coat hanging on one of the dining room chairs, he felt a cool wave of relief wash over him. He'd been silly to worry about them. The men were simply sleeping off a hard night of drinking after all. Shaking his head at himself, he walked through the living room full of mismatched furniture and started to enter the short hallway, still calling out for the men, his footsteps seeming abnormally loud on the worn gray-and-black-spotted white tile. As he reached the corner of the hallway, though, Karnes stopped and looked down at something odd. There appeared to be a footprint on the hallway floor in what looked like blood. He knew it couldn't be that but wondered what might have made it. After looking at the reddish brown impression for a moment, Karnes continued on, trying to imagine where it could have come from.

A few steps into the hallway, though, he stopped suddenly, as if attached to a short tether. Karnes could see a pair of feet on the floor sticking out of the bathroom, a trail behind them of what he now admitted to himself was definitely blood. It looked to him as though someone bleeding pretty seriously had been dragged across the floor. After a second of confusion, Karnes crept over and peeked into the bathroom.

Karnes felt as if he had been suddenly transported into an especially gruesome horror movie. What he was seeing couldn't be real. He would later say of his discovery, "I couldn't believe what I saw. I couldn't believe it. It just wasn't human—I still can't believe it."

Lying faceup on the red and pink shag rug, hands and ankles bound, was the body of James Barker. A huge pool of blood, from what appeared to be gaping cuts across his throat, circled his head. Spatters of more blood, looking like some grotesque modern art exhibit, covered the toilet, sink, bathtub, and nearby walls.

Horror etched on his face, Karnes quickly backed away from the bathroom and then stumbled down the hallway. In the back bedroom at the northwest corner of the house he found another grotesque sight: Robert Gierse, lying faceup on the bed, also bound at the hands and ankles, and also with a slit throat that had gushed blood all over his dark pink shirt and onto the bed around him. As in the bathroom, large spatters of blood covered the walls, while a dark red pool of congealed blood surrounded Gierse's head. Gierse, he could see, wore a gag made of what appeared to be torn cloth.

His stomach lurching, Karnes turned and again stumbled back down the hallway, trying to get away from the gruesome sights. But when Karnes looked into the bedroom at the northeast corner of the house, at the other end of the hallway, the nightmare continued. Although he had already seen similar sights twice, seeing it a third time didn't make it any less horrific. Sprawled facedown on the bed, pieces of a torn cloth binding his hands behind him and his ankles together, lay Robert Hinson. Karnes gulped for air as he stared at the splatters of blood on the pink walls and then looked unbelieving at the huge pool of congealed blood that surrounded Hinson's face and had soaked his blue shirt and suede jacket.

The brutality of what he had found seemed unbelievable, and at first, Karnes didn't know what to do. He had no life experiences to show him how to deal with this. Nothing in his life thus far had prepared him for this kind of situation. He only wanted to get away, to escape from the horror he had stumbled into, and so finally he turned and simply ran. But when he reached the front door, Karnes stopped. He knew he needed to call the police. They would know what to do. With numb, fumbling fingers, he turned around and picked up the house telephone, calling the Indianapolis Police Department.

Yet, when Karnes, in a frightened, stammering voice, told the police dispatcher what he had found in the house on North LaSalle Street, the dispatcher initially didn't believe him. Even though in 1971 Indianapolis had a population of nearly three quarters of a million people, it didn't have crime like this. Nothing so horrible and brutal had ever happened there. Indianapolis had had

plenty of murders over the years, but nothing as gruesome as this. Crime like that only happened in other
cities. Karnes, the dispatcher thought, was probably just
a crank caller. For a moment, the dispatcher considered
simply disregarding his call. However, realizing what
would happen if he was wrong, and thinking better of
it, the dispatcher decided to be safe. He contacted Indianapolis police officer Michael Williams, who patrolled
the area around North LaSalle Street, and told him to
Signal Three (call the dispatcher by telephone). When
Officer Williams did, the dispatcher told him what the
caller had claimed. Even though the dispatcher said it
was likely just a crank call, he asked Officer Williams to
drive by and check out the situation.

A few minutes later, Officer Williams pulled his blue
and white police car up to 1318 North LaSalle Street. He
saw Karnes standing on the porch. Karnes was waving
frantically and shouting, "In here! In here!" Officer Williams began to suspect that perhaps the dispatcher was
wrong, that maybe something bad had happened after all.

Less than a minute later, Officer Williams raced out of
the house and back to his patrol car. Gasping for breath,
Williams shouted into his radio microphone, "Send
me Car Eighty-three! Send me Identification! Send me a
coroner! Send me a superior officer! We've got a triple
murder!"

Officer Larry Summers was nearby and would answer
the call. Because it was his assigned beat, he would make
the original Teletype report on the triple murder, which
would be designated 786420-D.

As is common with incidents of a particularly gruesome or spectacular nature, the police began to arrive in
droves, crowding the street with their patrol cars. Nothing like this had ever happened in Indianapolis before,
and they all wanted to see it. Firemen at a nearby fire-
house, hearing the call and thinking that perhaps the
officer could be wrong and that someone who needed
medical help might still be alive inside the house, rushed
over in their fire engine.

News reporters also picked up the call and hurried to
the scene, cameras and notebooks in hand. Following
them were crowds of curious people who began collecting in front of the house, having heard about the incident
over their police scanners or on the local radio and television news. Others came, too: individuals who knew or
had worked with the three men, such as their secretary,
Louise Cole, and Diane Horton, who was dating Gierse
at the time. As might be expected from all of this, a cir-
cuslike atmosphere soon enveloped the neighborhood.

Deputy Chief of Investigations Ralph Lumpkin, who
also came to the scene, couldn't believe what he saw
when he looked around inside the house. He immediately called and ordered police department technicians
to bring out the video equipment to record the murder scene. Video recording was brand-new technology in
1971, and this incident became the first murder scene
ever videotaped by the Indianapolis Police Department.

Taking charge of the crime scene, Chief Lumpkin
quickly assigned Detective Lieutenant Joseph McAtee to
head up the homicide team that would investigate the

murders. He knew this incident would gather lots of media attention, and he wanted the best people possible to investigate this case. McAtee, a tall, thin man whose features seemed to be all sharp angles, was a top detective who always surrounded himself with competent, dedicated, and hardworking people—a quality that would eventually carry him up through the ranks of the police department to the chief of police's job, then on to becoming the sheriff of Marion County. McAtee selected Detective Sergeants Michael Popcheff and James Strode to work with him on the North LaSalle Street case.

Popcheff, young, athletic, with dark hair, liked to play golf and dress well. But he was also known as an excellent and hardworking investigator. Strode, a redhead a bit older than Popcheff, took homicide investigation as seriously as any man in the police department. He was known to throw himself totally into cases. Both men, McAtee knew, were tough, experienced investigators he could depend on.

Strangely enough, when Popcheff and Strode arrived at the scene, they remembered having been to the house on North LaSalle Street on a murder case before. Six months earlier, they had come to see if Gierse and Hinson had any information about the murder of a salesman who had provided microfilm and equipment to them. The twenty-five-year-old salesman, John Terhorst, had been shot twice in the head at close range in March 1971, and then dumped into Eagle Creek on the northwest side of Indianapolis. Terhorst had worked for E. I. du Pont de Nemours and Company out of Chicago, and had first met the three murdered men when they were living and working in Chicago. On the day of his murder, Terhorst told a close acquaintance that he was headed to the Woodruff Place neighborhood on the east side of Indianapolis to see a man named Bobby, who was interested in buying his 1966 black Corvette. Although the police found Terhorst's body, they never found his Corvette. As of December 1, 1971, the Terhorst case was still unsolved.

"We were at the house six months earlier on the John Terhorst investigation," said Popcheff. "They were having a cookout and saw us coming. Gierse told everyone that he would do the talking, which he did."

As the investigation into the triple murder progressed and became more complex, McAtee would later add Detective Sergeants Pat Stark and Bob Tirmenstein to the investigative team. Stark, middle-aged and totally bald, was a veteran homicide detective who eventually became the National Fraternal Order of Police president from 1975 to 1979. Tirmenstein, also older and a veteran detective, would work his way up to the rank of captain and was in charge of the Special Investigations Branch before succumbing to cancer in the 1990s.

After McAtee, Popcheff, and Strode had heard from Officer Williams concerning what he'd found inside the house, they realized this wouldn't be a pretty case, but likely an easily solvable one. Anyone who would kill three men so brutally obviously had a terrible grudge against them. That kind of rage typically couldn't be suppressed or hidden for long. And so, with just a little investigation, they figured, they ought to be able to locate this person and close the case. The killer, they assumed, would have to have made his anger known to someone. With this thought in mind, McAtee and his team mounted the front steps of 1318 North LaSalle and got ready for their initial walk-through of the crime scene.

CHAPTER TWO

"Oh my God!" were the first words uttered by most of those who visited the crime scene on North LaSalle Street. The *Indianapolis Star* would call them "the most vicious crimes ever committed in Indianapolis."

Throughout their careers, Lieutenant Joe McAtee and his team of homicide investigators had been to the scene of hundreds of homicides—but none of them had ever seen anything like this. Although there had been many murders in Indianapolis in the years before, no one could recall a case even close to as brutal as this one. Everywhere one of the detectives turned in the house, it seemed, there lay a body, its head yanked back at an unnatural angle, blood settling around the head in huge coagulated puddles.

"The scene was the worst I'd ever seen because of the way they killed them," said Popcheff. "They cut their necks all the way through. Another cut and their heads would have come off. That bothered me for quite a while, thinking about it."

While the detectives would have liked to have started their investigation with a pristine crime scene, that didn't happen. Because the crime had been so unusual and so gruesome, other officers, mostly high-ranking ones, had wanted to see what had happened—so despite protocol, these other officers had wandered through the house and looked around before the homicide detectives could get there and take control of the scene.

"Jim Strode and I were meticulous about securing the crime scene," said Popcheff. "But when we got there we found there'd already been people in the house before us, and that really disappointed us."

They were especially disappointed because later in their search the detectives would find that they had to be extremely careful where they stepped or what they brushed against. Surfaces everywhere had blood spattered on them. There was blood on the floors, on the walls, on the furniture, on the curtains, on the fixtures, and on the clothing that lay scattered all around the house. The detectives doubted that those in the house before them had been that careful. They could only imagine how much evidence had been trampled on, brushed against, or displaced. But there was nothing they could do about it by then. It was too late.

At any homicide scene, the homicide investigators' first step—as it was even in 1971—is to conduct a very careful initial walk-through to evaluate the scene, attempt to develop a working theory about what happened, and mark any evidence that the crime lab needs to process and collect. These walk-throughs aren't intended to solve the crime, though that does occasionally happen. Rather, they're simply meant to acquaint the detectives with what they have and what they will need to properly process the crime scene and, unless they have already received reliable information about what happened, to allow them to develop a working, tentative theory about what occurred. This theory must be very flexible, however, so that it can be changed if necessary with each new discovery of evidence. A more solid theory about what happened won't come until after all of the evidence has been collected and preliminary interviews conducted.

The detectives began their initial walk-through on North LaSalle Street in the living room, and they could see right away that the home had all the markings of a bachelor pad. No woman, they knew, would have decorated a house like this. The room was unorganized; the furniture was all mismatched. As they looked around, the detectives saw a plaid padded chair with clothing lying draped across a worn ottoman sitting in front of it, a flowery wingback, and two couches that didn't match anything else. On a beat-up and scarred coffee table sat a collection of empty Stroh's beer bottles, while under the table rested several empty pizza boxes. Shoes and clothing lay scattered all around the living room. But notably, the messy living room didn't show any signs of a struggle: no overturned or broken furniture.

The living room also had two televisions—a color

console television and a smaller portable one sitting on top of it (the console would later be reported to be stolen). Between the front door and the plaid chair sat a large roll of Owens Corning fiberglass insulation with a newspaper resting on top of it, looking like a makeshift end table. Friends would tell the police that Gierse had had plans to install it soon, though it had been sitting there for a while.

During the initial look at the room, the detectives found both Gierse's and Hinson's wallets. Gierse's lay on the floor and Hinson's on the coffee table. The detectives would also later find a watch belonging to Gierse stuffed down into the cushions of a couch. Was this just an accidental drop, they wondered, or had he put it there to keep it from being taken? The possibility of robbery as a motive suddenly found its way into the working theory. On the floor in front of one of the couches the detectives spied a set of keys. They also noticed a tape recorder in the living room. It had a tape in it, so the detectives marked it to be taken as evidence. Although the detectives knew it was unlikely, it might contain evidence of the crime.

As they continued their initial walk-through of the house, Popcheff and Strode discovered a drop of blood on the floor in a dining area that sat between the living room and the kitchen, showing that the killer had likely passed this way afterward, possibly to leave by the back door. They marked the blood for processing by the crime lab technicians. The detectives also found a potential clue in the dining area, a cigar in an ashtray, a clue that they never released to the public. (It is common practice to keep a few details from public knowledge, to help separate true culprits from those who, for various reasons, falsely confess.)

"There was a big ashtray in the dining room that had a cigar butt in it," said Popcheff. "Someone had laid a cigar in the ashtray and none of the three guys smoked cigars."

The detectives, after passing through the small dining area, stepped into the kitchen, where they saw that the counter held numerous liquor bottles and a box that had once contained a thirty-two-piece glass tumbler set. The ironing board and iron were still set up as if someone had just used them. The trash can sat filled with empty beer containers and whiskey bottles. It didn't take much of a detective to figure out that either the people who lived here liked to entertain a lot or were some really heavy drinkers. The police would later discover that both were true.

Walking over to the back door, which led out of the kitchen and onto the back porch, the detectives found that the door sat slightly ajar, but hadn't been forced. The working theory now included the murderer or murderers possibly entering and likely leaving this way. As a part of their investigation, the detectives would later examine all of the windows in the house, and although several of them were unlocked, the dust patterns around them hadn't been disturbed, indicating that no one had entered or exited through them. A much more thorough search of the house, including the full attic and half basement, showed no signs of a forced entry anywhere. The detectives now added another question to be answered about the murders: How did the front and rear doors get unlocked? This wasn't the kind of neighborhood where people would have left their doors unlocked at night.

McAtee and his crew left the kitchen, passed back through the dining area, and then walked through a door that led to a hallway that ran along the north side of the house. The hallway, they found, ran from a bedroom on the east to another on the west, with a bathroom between them. The sheared-copper smell of blood was so bad on the north side of the house that it made the detectives' eyes water. When the detectives reached the bedroom at the northeast corner of the house, they looked in to see Robert Hinson lying facedown on the bed, his arms and legs bound with a piece of torn cloth, later found to be part of a bedsheet, a gag made of the same material tied across his mouth. Hinson, the detectives could see, wore blue-and-gray-checked slacks and a blue shirt. But more important to the detectives was the tan imitation suede jacket he wore, indicating to them that he had just come in from the outside when attacked. Blood from his severe throat wound soaked the sheets and quilt he lay on.

As their gaze moved around the room, the detectives spied a set of blood-spattered clothes draped across a chair next to Hinson's feet. But then they also noticed that two drawers of a dresser next to the chair stood open, again bringing up the possibility of robbery as a motive.

The detectives, upon closer inspection of the room, found that the dresser, along with the blue window curtains, had been spattered with blood. They also found blood on the floor next to the dresser and on the east and south walls. Also on the floor, they discovered, lay a pillow with a large glob of blood on it. The victim, they figured, had apparently put up a struggle before being killed. While the science of blood spatter analysis wouldn't be fully developed until years later, the detectives could tell that the violence in this room had been tremendous.

"Whoever killed Hinson pulled his head up and sliced his throat so violently that the blood sprayed off the blade and onto the wall," said Popcheff.

"We've got a nasty one; this is really messy," one of the detectives would tell reporters.

As the detectives left the room, they stepped carefully when they saw drops of blood leading out of the bedroom and down the hallway, possibly having dripped off of the murder weapon. As they approached the next room, a bathroom, they spied an important piece of evidence in the hallway: a shoe or boot print on the tile floor. Someone, they could see, had stepped in the blood and left a mark. The pattern, a diamond design, appeared to the detectives to have likely come from a boot or overshoe. The detectives immediately marked the print for processing by the crime lab. This would be a key piece of evidence that could tie someone to the crime scene.

While most people might think that a murderer would immediately get rid of the shoes or boots worn at the scene of the crime, this doesn't happen as often as might be expected. Sometimes the murderer doesn't realize that he stepped in the blood, sometimes he's just lazy, but quite often the murderer won't get rid of the evidence because he doesn't want to have to buy new boots or shoes. Many murders over the years have been solved with evidence like this, so the detectives felt good about finding it.

Inside the bathroom, the detectives found another man, later identified as James Barker, lying on his back, also bound hand and foot. Unlike the man in the front bedroom, however, Barker's hands had been bound with a piece of cord, possibly taken from a venetian blind. Like the man in the front bedroom, Barker's feet were tied together with cloth, but in this case the killer had used a man's shirt with a French cuff to secure his legs. The detectives found another piece of torn cloth, also likely from a bedsheet, around Barker's neck. They believed that it had been used as a gag, but was now loose, again suggesting a struggle. These men, the detectives realized, hadn't meekly submitted to being killed, but had clearly fought back, making the absence of overturned or broken furniture even more puzzling.

Barker wore brown slacks and a green shirt, but he also wore his jacket, a tan Windbreaker, as if, like Hinson, he'd been attacked just as he came in from outside. It would later be found that the killer had wiped the knife or other cutting instrument on Barker's jacket. Barker's left pants pocket appeared to have been pulled out, once more raising the possibility of robbery as a motive for the murders. Barker's head lay next to a cast-iron freestanding bathtub that someone had decorated with three eagle decals, his feet sticking out of the door into the hallway. Similar to Hinson, Barker had apparently died from a severe slashing to his throat.

The bathroom floor had a red and pink shag carpet that had now soaked up the blood from the gaping wounds to Barker's throat. Also, the detectives noticed, blood had been spattered onto a cabinet, the toilet, the bathtub, and the green and white tile walls. All of this blood, everywhere, again showed the detectives that these men had fought back pretty strenuously, even if unsuccessfully. Upon inspecting the room, the detectives found a half-empty blood-spattered pack of Salem cigarettes next to the toilet and a Zayre's department store paper cup next to Barker's head. A checkbook belonging to Barker lay on the floor next to the victim's right leg. The detectives wondered if it had been dropped by the murderer or had fallen out of Barker's pocket during the struggle.

In the final bedroom, at the northwest corner of the house, the detectives found the body of Robert Gierse lying faceup on a bed covered with a blood-soaked yellow sheet. The room, with its walls painted blue, looked typical of a single man. Clothes had been strewn onto a chair just inside the door, and some also lay on the floor.

On the dresser sat a doll wearing a party hat, along with an empty can of Pabst Blue Ribbon beer.

Upon examining the area of the bed around the body, the detectives could see a blood pattern suggesting that the murderer had wiped the blade off on the sheet. The sheet also appeared to have been slashed in several places.

"They cut Gierse's throat so fast and so hard that whoever did it also cut the sheet after it [the blade] went through his neck," said Popcheff. "Then they went to the end of the bed to wipe off the knife and cut the sheet. That's how sharp the blade was."

Gierse lay with his hands under his back, and when he was eventually turned over, the detectives found that his hands had been bound with cord similar to that used on Barker. His feet had been tied together by more pieces of a torn bedsheet. Unlike the other two victims, Gierse didn't have his jacket on, but wore a dark pink shirt and gray slacks, suggesting to the detectives that he had been inside the house for at least several minutes before the murderer attacked him. (The detectives would later find Gierse's coat hung up in the hall closet.) A gag, also made of a piece of torn cloth, covered Gierse's mouth, while a huge amount of blood had flowed onto the bed from the gaping wound to his throat. In his shirt pocket the detectives discovered a silver ring, while on the floor the detectives found a T-shirt and three rags covered with blood. The murderer, the detectives suspected, had possibly used these to clean up something. Interestingly, it appeared that an item had been taken off of the nightstand in Gierse's bedroom. The detectives knew they needed to find out what it was.

The homicide team's initial examination of the murder scene indicated to them that the three men had almost certainly died from huge blood loss due to the cuts on their throats, which would eventually be found to be so deep that the men's spines had all been sliced. Later investigation would show that, after being bound, the three men had likely been grabbed and held by the hair, their necks stretched taut, as their throats were cut. The police would also later find that Hinson had broken the bonds on his hands, apparently in an unsuccessful attempt to fight off his attacker.

Despite the initial speculation that robbery might have played a part, a cursory look around the house on North LaSalle Street showed the detectives that robbery didn't appear to be the motive for the murders after all. There were no signs of forced entry anywhere. Nothing of value in the house appeared to have been taken or disturbed, and the men's wallets still contained money. Nor could the detectives find any signs of a struggle in the house; no overturned or broken furniture, as there surely would have been for a home-invasion type of robbery. No, the motive very likely lay elsewhere.

The detectives could clearly see that the method of killing the three men had been especially bloody and gruesome. Was this, they wondered, supposed to be some sort of sign or warning? If so, to whom? Regardless, the means of killing indicated that the murderer had harbored an intense anger against the three men. Had the victims heard the others being butchered, knowing that they would be next? That could explain the signs of frantic struggling against their bindings. In addition, the detectives wondered why the men had allowed themselves to be tied up in the first place. Had they thought the murderer only meant to rob them and discovered too late that they had been wrong?

Rigor mortis had set in on all of the bodies by the time the police did their initial walk-through. This meant that the murders had occurred at least twelve hours earlier. So although the bodies were discovered on the afternoon of December 1, the date of death Deputy Coroner Dr. H. S. Esparza would later list for the men was November 30, 1971. (However, this date would have the notation "approx" after it.)

Despite how variables such as air temperature, heavy clothing, body weight, and so forth can affect the timing, under normal conditions a dead body becomes fully rigid from rigor mortis about twelve hours after death, then stays that way for twenty-four to thirty-six hours before the stiffness disappears. So, while not precise to the minute, rigor mortis can be useful in helping homicide detectives establish an approximate time of death (which can then be used in conjunction with other evidence to give a more exact time).

For example, the detective's later refined theory about time of death was that, since Gierse and Hinson still wore the same clothing witnesses had seen them in the day before, the two men had likely been killed as they came home from work late the previous evening. Their secretary, Louise Cole, told police that Gierse and Hinson had intended to work until at least 7:30 or 8:00 P.M., but they may have decided to stay later.

The detectives believed that Gierse, since he had hung his coat up in the hall closet, had likely arrived home before Hinson, who may have stopped somewhere first. Barker, they believed, arrived last. The positions of the men's cars parked in front of the house supported this theory. Gierse and Hinson had parked their cars on the east side of North LaSalle Street facing north, as they would have done if they were just returning home from their office on East 10th Street. Gierse's car was parked first with Hinson's car behind him. Barker had parked his car on the west side of North LaSalle Street facing south, meaning that he had likely come from the direction of his home on North Rural Street. The detectives believed that the men had been confronted one after another as they arrived at the house, bound in different rooms, and then murdered.

Once the initial walk-through had been completed, crime lab technicians began processing the crime scene, paying particular attention to the objects the detectives had marked. One of their first tasks was to collect samples of blood from all of the rooms. As the homicide detectives knew, often when the murder weapon is a knife or other sharp object, a killer may cut himself while stabbing and slashing, and leave some of his own blood at the scene. Although DNA analysis wasn't yet available in 1971, blood typing and other markers in the blood could still help point to a suspect.

Additionally, most murders are committed impulsively, by amateur killers, not professional hit men. Consequently, a murderer who perhaps had not originally planned on killing anyone will often flee the scene immediately afterward, leaving fingerprints behind. And even if they do think to wipe off some objects, impulsive killers can seldom remember everything they've touched. Also, in 1971 there were not any television programs such as *CSI* to educate the public about the evidence police technicians can obtain from a crime scene. Far fewer laymen back then knew anything about the process of forensics.

The homicide investigators had the crime lab dust for fingerprints on dozens of objects in the house on North LaSalle, including a large number of beer bottles. Technicians found and recovered fingerprints from an ashtray, inside the front door glass, on several of the empty Stroh's beer bottles, on a scotch bottle found in the kitchen, on three drinking glasses sitting in the living room, on the doors and door moldings of the bedrooms and bathroom, on a telephone in one of the bedrooms, on a Stroh's eight-pack container, and on a Michelob beer bottle. The technicians also recovered fingerprints from each of the men's cars parked in front of the house, which the detectives had them check in case one of the victims had possibly brought the murderer home with him, not knowing his intention.

There was one fingerprint recovered in particular that detectives thought, like the footprint in the hallway, could give them a solid lead. "We had a really good fingerprint that we thought might belong to the killer," said Popcheff. "But our fingerprint man carried it around with him rather than keeping it in the file, and when he died the fingerprint disappeared."

This wasn't as odd as it might seem; the fingerprint technician kept the print on him so that he could compare it against every new fingerprint that came in. But, of course, this was not a secure way to store fingerprints. Fortunately, all of the other unidentified fingerprints from the case had been stored in the file, so no others were lost.

Along with the problem of the lost fingerprint, another problem concerning the fingerprints loomed. Even though the technicians had recovered many fingerprints, in precomputer 1971 the recovery of fingerprints at a crime scene held little value unless the detectives had a known suspect whose prints they could compare them against. If fingerprints arose in an investigation that didn't match any of those of the known suspects, they simply went into the file. In those days, there was simply no practical way to compare an unknown fingerprint against the millions of fingerprints already on file. Still, fingerprints were recovered and kept, to be compared against those of any future suspects that might be developed in the case.

Many years later, the police department did run all of the unidentified fingerprints from the North LaSalle

Street murders through its Automated Fingerprint Identification System (AFIS), a piece of technology not available until the mid-1980s. AFIS is a complex computer system that digitizes fingerprints and then stores this digitized information in its memory. When a fingerprint taken from a crime scene is entered into AFIS, the computer digitizes the evidentiary fingerprint and then compares it with the millions of fingerprints in its memory. It takes only minutes to compare them, whereas in the past, manually comparing these fingerprints would have taken years.

AFIS's popularity rose dramatically when in 1985 the Los Angeles Police Department used one of the country's first AFIS systems to identify a fingerprint taken from a stolen car. The fingerprint belonged to the infamous Night Stalker, a criminal deviant who had killed over a dozen people and raped countless women in a yearlong crime spree. The AFIS system showed that the fingerprint belonged to a man named Richard Ramirez, and the police were able to apprehend Ramirez soon after.

The FBI, in order to assist local police departments in nationwide identification, maintains a link among all of the police AFIS computers across the United States. Consequently, a person arrested and fingerprinted in Indianapolis could match a fingerprint recovered from a crime in Seattle. However, regardless of this system's potential, there was ultimately no match in AFIS for the unidentified fingerprints from North LaSalle Street.

This crime scene, because it had three separate murder locations, took much longer than most ordinary homicide scenes to process. Each body had to be examined for evidence, as did the area surrounding the bodies. The detectives and crime lab personnel were at the house for hours. During their search of the crime scene, the homicide detectives found an address book containing the usual collection of names, addresses, and telephone numbers; but this one also listed dozens of women's first names. This would turn out to be the scorecard of the three men's sex contest. The detectives took the address book along as evidence, figuring it as important, but not yet knowing just how big a part it would eventually play in the investigation.

While the homicide detectives were at the house conducting their walk-through, they received telephone calls from several people who had heard the news and simply couldn't believe it was true—including, ironically, a call from an insurance agent who was in the process of writing life insurance policies for Gierse and Hinson. Also, the news of this killing apparently soon reached beyond Indianapolis. The following day, Paula Palmer, Jim Barker's ex-wife, who lived in Chicago, called the Homicide Office. Although Palmer and Jim had been out with the other two victims many times while they were married, she couldn't provide the detectives with much information regarding a potential motive or pinpoint any specific person who might want to murder the three men.

Quite often, as the detectives knew, a motive for a murder can be found in the lifestyle of murder victims. The places they visited, the acquaintances they made, and the activities they became involved in could often help homicide detectives determine why they were murdered and likely by whom. And so homicide investigators often research the victims and their lifestyles, looking for clues as to who would want to murder them. In this case, the police would eventually find that *plenty* of people wanted to murder these three men.

Robert Gierse, six feet two inches tall and 215 pounds, was the oldest of the three victims at thirty-four. Friends would later tell the police that when Gierse got his first job in the microfilm business, he found that he loved the field and never left it. Originally from St. Louis, Gierse had come to Indianapolis by way of Chicago, where he'd been employed by the Bell and Howell Company. When he arrived in Indianapolis in 1967 he and Hinson had roomed together in New Augusta, then a northwest-side suburb of Indianapolis. He initially got a job with Commercial Microfilm Services, Inc., and worked there for a year or so before moving on to the Records Security Corporation, where he quickly became executive vice president and general manager, making $225 a week, a decent salary in the late 1960s. Those in the microfilming business saw Gierse as a rising star, and at every place he worked his bosses described him as knowledgeable and extremely hardworking.

A month or so before his murder, Gierse had left Records Security Corporation to start his own business with Bob Hinson: B&B Microfilming Service Company.

Detectives would later find that when Gierse left his job at Records Security Corporation, he took several of his previous employer's best customers with him to B&B.

Like Barker, Gierse was divorced. He had served in the army from 1955 to 1962. Friends reported that he had a photographic memory and was a very smooth and convincing speaker, which helped him in his near-constant womanizing. Acquaintances also said that he could really hold his liquor, and that, even though a diabetic, he and his two friends, Hinson and Barker, drank a lot.

Robert Hinson, twenty-seven years old, was also six feet two inches tall (though forty pounds heavier than Gierse), and originally hailed from Wilson, North Carolina. He had proven numerous times to be very good with his fists, which he'd had to use often, given the many scraps the three men got themselves into as they prowled low-class bars and flirted with other men's girlfriends and wives. Hinson had worked with Gierse at Bell and Howell in Chicago before also coming to Indianapolis and working for Commercial Microfilm Services. But then, like Gierse, he had ended up at Records Security Corporation, which he left in September 1971, a couple of months before Gierse, to start up B&B Microfilming Service Company.

Although not as smooth a talker as Gierse, Hinson had no problem finding plenty of women to sleep with—unfortunately, often to the chagrin of their husbands and boyfriends. Like his two friends, Hinson was divorced and loved to drink and party. He'd served in the navy from 1961 to 1965, and like Gierse, his employers described him as knowledgeable and a hard worker.

James Barker, twenty-seven years old, was the youngest of the trio (five months younger than Hinson, but an inch taller and fifteen pounds lighter). Originally from West Virginia, he had played football in high school and graduated from Wright Junior College in Chicago. He had also come to Indianapolis through Chicago, but, unlike Gierse and Hinson, he still worked for Bell and Howell, based in Indianapolis as a service manager, making $220 a month plus bonuses. Friends would say that in the months before his murder he had talked about leaving Bell and Howell, which was considering cutting his salary, and going into business with Gierse and Hinson at B&B Microfilming.

Barker had served in the army as a military policeman from 1966 to 1968. Very much like Gierse and Hinson, Barker liked the ladies and had plenty of feminine company. Barker also liked to drink and party, and did a lot of it with his two friends.

While Lieutenant McAtee and his team were inside the house conducting their investigation, outside on the street in front of the house, a crowd of spectators had congregated. Because the murders were so unusual and horrific, the news media coverage of them began almost immediately. The breaking television and radio broadcasts drew dozens of curious people there. A tactic the police often used in cases like this was to have several plainclothes police officers walk through the crowd, trying to pick up what the people were saying about the crime. Leads to suspects could often be developed this way.

In this case, however, it wasn't a police officer but a reporter who overheard two women talking. Bill Anderson of the *Indianapolis Star*, the city's morning newspaper, heard a woman say, "Do you think J.T. did this?" and the other respond, "I don't know. He may have. He was mad." The women, as it turned out, were talking about a man named James T. Cole, whose wife, Louise, worked as the secretary at B&B Microfilming. The police would later receive reports from witnesses that Mr. Cole suspected his wife of having an affair with one of the three men.

Other detectives assisted McAtee and his team by interviewing people about the case and compiling a list of persons of interest who would be taken downtown for further questioning. This list included several girlfriends of the three victims. The detectives also began compiling a preliminary list of possible suspects, including James T. Cole and a man named Bob Romine, whom witnesses told detectives they'd seen driving Gierse's Cadillac. Another of the suspects was Carroll Horton, whose ex-wife, Diane Horton, had been dating Gierse at the time of his murder.

"While we were in the crime scene an officer came in and said that a man had to see me right away," said Popcheff. "I went out, and standing on the other side of the crime scene barrier was Carroll Horton. He told me that these guys were working with some kind of secret papers. We kept hearing that they were supposed to have been microfilming secret documents. But we never could find any." This idea of the victims being involved in micro-filming secret documents, though it wouldn't be connected to the murders in 1971, would resurface some years later.

While talking to witnesses at the scene, the assisting detectives also discovered a tidbit about the three men that they felt warranted further investigation. Witnesses told the police how the murdered men, on the night before their deaths, had gotten into a heated argument with three other men at the Idle Hour Tavern, allegedly over a woman one of them had flirted with. Later that night, witnesses told the detectives, Hinson had also administered a beating to another man at the Hi Neighbor Tavern, again allegedly over a woman. The detectives recorded this information as good leads for McAtee and his team to follow up on.

Once the murder scene had been photographed and processed, and all of the available evidence recovered by the crime lab, McAtee had a coroner's seal put on the house on North LaSalle Street, as well as on the business office of B&B Microfilming Service Company on East 10th Street, and on Barker's home on North Rural Street. This crime scene had taken an extraordinarily long amount of time to process, but finally the detectives requested what was called in those days a B.I.D. (Brought in Dead) Wagon to take the bodies to the county morgue for autopsies.

The detectives sent the bodies to the morgue as they found them, still fully clothed and with their hands and feet still bound. They also called for wreckers to tow the men's vehicles to police headquarters so that they could be processed in a controlled location before being towed to a secure lot for storage.

After the crime scene, the next most valuable source of clues and evidence in any murder case is the autopsy, which in this case the coroner's office conducted on Thursday, December 2, 1971. Many times what looks like the cause of death actually isn't. This was true in the North LaSalle Street case. Anyone who had viewed the crime scene would likely have believed that the three men had died from a loss of blood. There were large puddles and spatters of it everywhere. That, however, wasn't the case. The coroner instead found that the injuries to the men's necks had been so severe that they had actually died from asphyxiation when their windpipes were severed.

"They didn't bleed to death," Marion County coroner Dennis Nichols would later state. "They asphyxiated when their windpipes and spinal columns were severed."

At the autopsy, the coroner discovered that Gierse, coroner's case #71-1215, in addition to the severe neck wound, also had three deep, straight-line lacerations—one of them 1 inch long, one of them 2½ inches long, and a third 3⅛ inches long—all on the right side of his head toward the rear. The coroner believed that these had come from him being struck with a tire iron or similar object. The homicide detectives would later theorize

that the killer or killers had tried to knock Gierse unconscious before cutting his throat. This would explain how
he had been tied up. Rather than meekly submitting,
which seemed unlikely at best, he had been knocked unconscious, only to regain consciousness too late.

Gierse's throat, the coroner found, had one smooth
and deep laceration 10¼ inches long. According to the
postmortem report, Gierse suffered a transection of the
larynx; carotid arteries, both sides; jugular veins, both
sides; and his esophagus. In addition to these injuries,
Gierse also had pressure marks on his stomach and wrists,
and a small laceration on his left knee. These last injuries, the detectives theorized, may well have come from
him struggling after he came to and realized what was
going to happen.

Hinson, coroner's case #71-1214, had two straight-
line lacerations to the right side of his head, one 3½
and the other 2½ inches long, and a laceration 1½ inches
long on the back of his head, again believed to have been
made by a tire iron or similar object. The coroner's examination found that the cut on Hinson's throat was
also smooth and deep, and 7 inches long, situated ½ inch
below his Adam's apple. According to the postmortem
report, Hinson suffered a transection of the larynx, right
carotid artery, right jugular vein, and right sternocleido-
mastoid muscle. The coroner also noted in his report that
Hinson had two tattoos, one on each shoulder: flowers
on his left shoulder and the name Geri (his ex-wife) on
his right shoulder.

Like the other two men, Barker, coroner's case

#71-1216, had three straight-line lacerations on his head, in his case all of them on the back, one of them 1¾ inches long, one 1½ inches long, and the other 1¼ inches long. But, unlike the others, Barker had been hit so hard that it fractured his skull. Also different from the other men, Barker had three lacerations to his throat, one 7½ inches long, one 5½ inches long, and the other 3 inches long. And rather than smooth cuts like the other two victims had, the coroner found that these lacerations were jagged, meaning that either the cutting instrument had dulled or that Barker had been struggling as it happened. The coroner also noticed two cuts on Barker's upper chest, one of them 4 inches long and the other 2 inches long, and a 2-inch-long cut on his stomach, again indicating that he had been struggling with his murderer. Barker additionally had deep ligament markings on his wrists and an abrasion over his right eye. According to the postmortem report, Barker suffered a transection of the pharynx; carotid arteries, both sides; and jugular veins, both sides.

The coroner in his examination could also see that all three of the men had been gripped by the hair to stretch their necks taut. In addition, as a part of his examination, the coroner took nail scrapings from each man in the event he had struggled with his assailant and scratched him, and took hair samples in the event other hairs would be found either on the men or at the crime scene.

All of this information from the coroner, of course, went into the homicide case file to be used in the ensuing investigation. But even this early in the case, when the detectives were just beginning to collect evidence and testimony, they quickly discovered that these three men, in their short lives, had made an amazing number of enemies. Their shared lifestyle of drinking, partying, and womanizing had angered hundreds of people, both male and female.

But the question was, who had been angry enough to kill them so brutally? This hadn't been an ordinary murder. It had been a massacre.

CHAPTER THREE

When Joe McAtee and his team of detectives arrived back at the Indianapolis Homicide Office the night of December 1, 1971, they felt more than optimistic about solving the murders on North LaSalle Street. The crime had certainly been violent and gruesome, but they knew that this fact could actually work to their advantage. The killer (or killers) had exhibited an intense rage against these three men that had burst loose and exploded into a bloody massacre, and that kind of uncontrolled anger isn't easy to hide. The killer would have to have shown some signs of this rage before the murders. The detectives felt confident that someone out there knew or suspected that a certain person was the killer. This person, they also felt confident, would likely soon tell someone else. Eventually, someone would tell the police, and the murderer would be uncovered.

Also, the murders had been so bloody that the killer had to have been covered with blood when he left. Very likely, the detectives knew, someone could have seen the killer with blood all over him, or the bloody clothing and shoes the killer wore. The detectives just needed to find this person.

In this case, the detectives had already drawn up a list of possible suspects whom they needed to bring in and question, either for a possible connection to the crime or to eliminate them as suspects. The detectives would also use this questioning as a means of gathering information and evidence that would point them toward more likely suspects.

In addition to conducting these interviews, homicide detectives needed to study the evidence recovered from the crime scene and during the autopsy. In this case, though, the crime scene and autopsy had provided very little physical evidence that could point toward the killer or killers. While the crime scene technicians had recovered a large number of fingerprints from the house, the detectives soon learned that there had been numerous parties held at the house, which meant that the fingerprints recovered could easily belong to one of the party-goers. And if the murderer or murderers had been in the home at one of these parties, then finding their fingerprints in the house would be of little or no value in the case.

The crime scene technicians had also recovered a large amount of blood from the house, as would be expected with murders so brutal, but since it was just the victims' blood, it didn't hold much evidentiary value. The only real piece of physical evidence the detectives had that could point specifically to one person as the killer was the bloody footprint in the hallway. The cigar in the dining room could at best only add a bit more support to the theory that a certain person was the killer. Detectives knew that they had to quickly narrow down their suspect list before the killer realized he needed to get rid of the footwear that had made the track in the blood.

While McAtee, Popcheff, and Strode had been busy at the crime scene, Detective Sergeants Pat Stark and Bob Tirmenstein, who were not yet assigned to the case but were still only assisting at this point, had brought in a group of people to be interviewed at police headquarters. This group included Louise Cole, the secretary at B&B Microfilming; her husband, James T. Cole; and John Karnes, the man who had reported the murders. Along with these individuals, the detectives also brought in the women each of the men had most recently been seeing: Bob Gierse's girlfriend, Diane Horton; Bob Hinson's girlfriend, Aleene Marcum; and Jim Barker's girlfriend, Wava Winslow. Someone in the group, the detectives believed, should have an idea of who would want to commit such a crime, or maybe would know of someone who had made a threat.

However, despite the detective's hopes, these individuals provided mostly only background information on the three men. Still, from these interviews the detectives did manage to compile a long list of other people who needed to be interviewed. For example, one of the interviewees told the detectives about a former girlfriend of Gierse's named Ilene Combest, who had supposedly gone to the house on North LaSalle Street, extremely upset at having been two-timed by Gierse, and had ended up making a scene and breaking the glass in the front door. Would this be enough to make someone want to commit such a brutal triple murder? Probably not, the detectives thought, but still it merited looking into.

During her interview with the detectives, Gierse's girlfriend Diane Horton added corroboration to the time of death timeline by stating how, on the way home from a girlfriend's house, she had driven by the North LaSalle Street address at around 1:00 A.M. on December 1. She had hoped to stop by for a while but said that although she saw all three of the men's cars there, no lights were on in the house, so instead of stopping she drove on.

Louise Cole, the secretary at B&B Microfilming and a mother of seven children, told the detectives how B&B, even in its very short span of business, had already established an impressive list of customers, a number of whom the company had taken away from Gierse and Hinson's previous employer, Records Security Corporation. All of the people interviewed said that the three men were inseparable and had gotten along remarkably well. They never seemed to tire of one another or have personal spats. Friends called them the Three Musketeers.

Strangely enough, on Thursday, December 2, 1971,

the day following her interview at police headquarters, Mrs. Cole called the police and told officers that at around 6:00 A.M. that day she had received a telephone call at her unlisted number. She didn't recognize the caller, who had asked to speak to her husband. When James Cole got on the line, he said the caller told him that he would be the next one to be murdered.

The Coles' story might have seemed far-fetched or paranoid, but while the police were at the Cole house taking the report, the couple received several more telephone calls, which one of the police officers monitored. In one of these calls, the caller made threats against Mrs. Cole's life, and in another the caller made obscene remarks about the Coles' fourteen-year-old daughter. A further caller told the Coles that the fire department was on the way (the fire department did indeed receive a false request to go there), while another caller threatened to kill both Mrs. Cole and her daughter. What was particularly odd was that the police officer monitoring the telephone said that the calls didn't seem to be coming from the same person. As might be imagined, these calls upset the Coles very much. They didn't know who these people were or how so many people had obtained their unlisted telephone number.

Also on December 2, 1971, Detective Sergeants Popcheff and Strode interviewed Ilene Combest, Gierse's former girlfriend. They found that, in a fit of jealousy over a woman named Brenda Wood, who was supposedly staying with Gierse, Combest had indeed thrown all of the woman's clothing out into the yard, and then broke the glass in the front door of the North LaSalle Street house. Combest said that she later felt bad about her behavior because Wood (who had been a secretary for Ted Uland, Gierse's former boss at Records Security Corporation) was actually a very nice person. Combest told the detectives that she had dated Gierse on and off for five years, and that the last time she'd had contact with him had been on the morning of November 30, 1971, the day he died.

Combest said she'd had a telephone conversation with Gierse at around 11:00 A.M. that day. Besides being lovers, they had also been friends, and so she asked him how his new business was going. He told her that they were doing great and that he had two garages full of file cabinets waiting to be microfilmed. He also told her that he'd just gotten the Indiana National Bank account, one of the largest banks in Indianapolis, and that he'd recently gotten a couple more accounts that had previously belonged to Records Security Corporation. He felt certain that B&B had a great future, and he was glad that he had left Records Security.

Besides being lovers and friends, Combest had also been a close confidant of Bob Gierse, who had told her about much of his business life. As a consequence, Combest was able to give the detectives some history on Records Security Corporation and its owner Ted Uland. A few years earlier, she said, Uland had had the opportunity to buy a bank vault in Logansport, Indiana, a small town a little over seventy miles north of Indianapolis.

The owner had offered it cheaply and so Uland bought it. But then, she said, he didn't know what to do with it until a friend told Uland about how the vault would be the perfect place to store microfilm. So Uland started up Records Security Corporation, which both microfilmed documents for companies and offered them secure storage for the microfilm.

At first, Combest told the detectives, Uland had a man named Henry Colchee running Records Security Corporation, but had reportedly fired him for stealing. Uland then hired Bob Gierse to take Colchee's place, and eventually, at Gierse's urging, he also hired Hinson. Once Colchee had been fired, Combest added, he was kind of left out in the cold with no job and little future. Wondering if this Colchee could be bitter about being fired and replaced by Gierse, detectives made a note to put him on their list of possible suspects.

When Uland hired Gierse at Records Security Corporation, Combest went on, the company had been experiencing serious financial problems because of unpaid taxes and a lot of misuse of money by Colchee. Uland expected Gierse to straighten it out. Along with microfilming, Uland had business interests in several other areas, his major business being digging oil wells, and so consequently, Uland had let Gierse essentially run Records Security Corporation until he quit to start up B&B Microfilming.

Combest then told the detectives how Hinson had quit Records Security Corporation first, but that Gierse had told her he was going to stay on until he could be sure that B&B would get several good contracts for microfilming. For a while Hinson ran B&B by himself. Combest said that for a time she had helped by answering the telephones for the business, which had been set up to ring at both the office on East 10th Street and at the house on North LaSalle Street. She said she asked Gierse if he thought that Records Security Corporation was going to be a lot of competition to them at B&B, but that Gierse had laughed and said no, since Uland didn't have a clue about what he was doing when it came to microfilming. She also later mentioned that Ted Uland and Richard Roller, a friend of the three men, both had keys to the house on North LaSalle Street. Why they did, no one knew.

The detectives, having heard hints and rumors from other individuals about a possible affair, also asked Ilene Combest about Bob Hinson's relationship with Louise Cole. Combest told the police that yes, she believed Hinson and Cole had been having an affair for several years, but that apparently Louise Cole had had no intention of divorcing her husband, with whom she'd had seven children. This was despite the fact that, according to Combest, James Cole had often threatened to beat his wife. There had even been an incident at a party once, she said, in which James, angry and suspicious as always, had poured a cup of coffee over Louise's head and made her cry.

When asked about other women the three men had dated, Combest told them about one of Gierse's girl-friends named Bonnie Russel, who had told several people at the beauty shop where Combest worked that the murders had been committed by the Mafia. She didn't say where this information had come from.

Finally, Combest told detectives about how she had heard from another person that Bob Gierse had once sent money to a woman named April Lynn Smoot when she and her husband, David Lynn, were stranded in New Orleans. Smoot had contacted Gierse and asked for his help, so he sent her $50. Smoot's husband, Combest said the person told her, became very suspicious and jealous, and accused her of having an affair with Gierse. He then reportedly blacked her eyes and threatened to kill all of them if April ever tried to leave him. The detectives made a note to add Mr. Lynn to their list of possible suspects, and, very important, to find out if April Lynn Smoot had recently been involved with Gierse.

Also on December 2, 1971, the detectives interviewed Sue Ross, the office manager at the Bell and Howell plant in Indianapolis, where James Barker had worked as a service manager. She said she had known all of the victims but hadn't dated any of them. Although the police had already learned about the men's lothario ways, Ross was the first person to mention the sex contest to the police, and it changed the direction of the investigation. She said Barker had told her about it. Suddenly, the detectives had a new motive and possibly dozens of new suspects. This information also gave new meaning to the list of women's names the detectives had found in the address book at the North LaSalle Street house.

The detectives knew this also meant they'd need to

find and interview dozens of new individuals in the case; not only the women involved in the sex contest, but potentially also their husbands or boyfriends. Any one of the women could have become angry at being used for the contest, or could have had a husband or boyfriend who found out about the contest and decided to seek revenge. But since the list only contained the first names of the women involved, or in some cases what appeared to be a nickname, the detectives could see hundreds of hours of work ahead trying to find these individuals.

And as if this thunderbolt of information didn't already add enough new suspects to the case, Ross added yet another to the detective's ever-growing list. As kind of an afterthought, she related how Barker had told her about an incident he and Bob Gierse had been involved in a couple of weeks earlier: Around the middle of November, Barker and Gierse had gone to a bar on East Washington Street and, while there, had gotten into an argument with a man who had ended up holding a knife to Barker's throat and telling him and Gierse to get out, which they did. Ross didn't know what the disagreement had been about, but chances were one of them had flirted with the man's wife or girlfriend. The detectives made a note to look further into this incident, too.

Another name that came from those initial interviews held on December 1 and 2 was Tim Ford. Detective Sergeants Popcheff and Strode found that Ford, who worked at a SupeRx Drug Store, had become acquainted with both Bob Gierse and Bob Hinson from riding motorcycles with them. He also independently corroborated Ilene Combest's belief that Hinson had been intimately involved with Louise Cole for some time. Ford said that he had attended Gierse's birthday party at the North La-Salle Street house on November 18 of that year, and that Louise and James Cole had also been there. A friend at the party, he said, told him that James Cole had been drinking heavily and was extremely angry and upset, telling the friend that he believed one of the three men was sleeping with his wife. Cole then told the friend that he would cut anyone he caught messing with his wife.

Following this bit of information, Ford recounted for the two detectives an incident that had occurred earlier in the year at a Knights of Columbus hall, in which James Cole had cut off Bob Gierse's tie with a knife. The detectives made a note to talk to Mr. Cole about these occurrences. He had suddenly moved up on the suspect list, especially when the detectives recalled the incident Bill Anderson, the reporter for the *Indianapolis Star*, had told them about in which two women in the crowd outside the North LaSalle Street house on the day of the murders discussed suspicions that Cole might be the murderer.

After talking to Ford, the detectives, again using information gained from other interviews, traveled to a home on West 26th Street in Indianapolis, where they spoke with a Mac and Laura Harbor, who also reportedly had information about the victims. This couple said that they, like Ford had said earlier, knew Gierse and Hinson from riding motorcycles with them. They also knew the Coles, and they said James was always suspicious that someone was messing with his wife. Like Ford, the Harbors had been present at the incident in which Cole had sliced off Gierse's tie.

Though not new, all this information confirmed the seriousness of James Cole as a key suspect. The Harbors said that they had also been at Gierse's birthday party. At that party, Mac said, he had been talking with James, who had been drunk. He said that James told him he was positive one of the three men was messing with his wife, and that if he could find out which one of the sons of bitches it was, he would cut his throat. Had Cole, the detectives wondered, found out which one he thought was having the affair with his wife? Or had he perhaps just decided to kill all three of them to be certain he got the right one? Popcheff and Strode knew that Cole had some serious explaining to do.

The detectives then drove back to the house on North LaSalle Street, where they met with Bob Gierse's brother Ted. Because the house had been sealed by the coroner, he needed their permission to go inside. Popcheff and Strode allowed him to go into the house to get a gray suit, white shirt, and pink-striped tie to use for Gierse's funeral. They also allowed Ted to take Gierse's Masonic apron from a dresser drawer so that it could be used during the Masonic ceremony at the funeral.

While there, the detectives took another look around the house, just to be absolutely certain they hadn't missed anything. Despite the very thorough search they had conducted on the day the murders had been discovered, the detectives knew that sometimes, once the bodies and other evidence had been removed, other items could stand out that hadn't seemed obvious the day of the initial investigation. Or, based on interviews with witnesses and persons of interest they'd since conducted, an item that hadn't appeared significant before could suddenly become key evidence. In this case, however, the detectives didn't find anything new.

The two detectives then drove to Jim Barker's house on North Rural Street to take another look around for any evidence they might have missed. But again, they didn't find anything of value. Barker's parents showed up while Popcheff and Strode were there, and after talking with them for a bit, the detectives called the coroner's office and had the house and its contents released to Barker's parents. The detectives had already searched the house twice, and since the murders had been committed somewhere else, they couldn't see any reason to keep the house sealed.

On the way back to police headquarters, Popcheff and Strode stopped off at the home of James and Louise Cole and requested they come back down for some more questioning. The detectives particularly wanted to confront Mr. Cole with the information about his threats to cut the throat of anyone he caught messing with his wife and see how he responded.

When the detectives arrived at police headquarters,

however, they first talked briefly with Barbara Munden, one of Bob Hinson's former girlfriends who had just been located. She said that she had started dating Hinson about two years earlier, and that she had gotten a divorce six months after that. She and Hinson had broken up two weeks before the murders because she said she had found a new boyfriend, who had since moved in with her. However, Munden also added that her new boyfriend had come home recently to find Hinson in her house. This added at least one more possible suspect—the new boyfriend—to the detectives' growing list; or maybe two, if the ex-husband had found out about the woman's affair with Hinson while they were still married.

Following this, Popcheff and Strode then began an in-depth interview with Louise Cole. She said that the last time she saw Gierse and Hinson had been at around 5:30 P.M. on Tuesday, November 30, 1971. She was leaving for home and they told her that they had some important microfilming to do and would be working late, probably until about 7:30 or 8:00 P.M. or even later. She then told the detectives that, like two of the murdered men, she had also previously worked for Records Security Corporation. She had gotten that job through Hinson, whom she had met at the Sherman Bar in Indianapolis. When Gierse and Hinson decided to leave Records Security Corporation and start their own business, they persuaded her to come and work for them at B&B Microfilming.

Mrs. Cole also told the detectives about an incident between Gierse and Ted Uland, the owner of Records

Security Corporation. She said that Gierse had a drawer in his house in which he kept all of his canceled checks, and that recently he had opened the drawer and found them missing. She said that Gierse told her he believed Uland, who had a key to the North LaSalle Street house, had come in and stolen the checks. Gierse was upset but didn't tell her why he thought Uland would want to do this.

In regards to her husband, Louise Cole told the detectives that on the night of the murders he had left home at around 7:40 P.M. and returned at about 9:30 P.M. She said she didn't know where he went but assured them he hadn't come back bloody. She would have noticed, she insisted—though of course, the detectives knew, he could have simply cleaned up before coming home. When asked if she would be willing to take a lie detector test, Louise agreed readily.

The polygraph, or lie detector, came into use in law enforcement in the 1920s. The device is meant to measure several physiological responses—such as perspiration, blood pressure, and pulse—as a person is asked a series of questions, the theory being that these measures will change when a person lies. Several contemporary studies, however, have since shown lie detectors to be only 80 to 90 percent effective; consequently, most courts won't allow their use as evidence. However, though much less likely to be used today, back in the early 1970s polygraphs were considered by the police to be much more reliable, and were often used to include or exclude someone as a suspect.

After this interview, the detectives talked to James Cole. They confronted him about his threats to cut the throat of anyone he caught messing with his wife. Cole at first denied knowing what they were talking about and claimed he had been too drunk to remember making this threat at Gierse's birthday party, but then finally said that, yes, he was a very jealous man and he might have said it. Apparently realizing where this was going, Cole then denied having anything to do with the North La-Salle Street murders, and when asked about the incident at the Knights of Columbus hall, he claimed that he had cut Gierse's tie off as a joke because the event was supposed to be casual. There had been no threat involved. It had all been in fun.

James Cole said that the last time he saw the three victims had been on November 25, Thanksgiving Day, when Bob Gierse had given the Coles an old Chevrolet he had. James said that on the night of the murders he left home around 7:30 P.M. and went to the Irvington Play Bowl, where he met up with some people he worked with, then stopped by a grocery store for a few minutes before returning home between 8:30 and 8:45 P.M. (about an hour earlier than his wife had said). He claimed that he knew what time it was when he got home because he got there in time to watch the television program *Hawaii Five-0*, which came on at 9:00 P.M. He couldn't, however, tell the detectives what the show had been about. When asked if he would be willing to take a lie detector test, he said he would, and the detectives—still listing him as a key suspect—decided to schedule it for as soon as possible.

After the questioning of Hinson's girlfriend and the Coles, Popcheff and Strode left police headquarters and, to close out the day, stopped by the Sherman Bar, which had been a popular hangout for the murdered men. A number of the people they'd interviewed had mentioned seeing or meeting the three victims there. At the bar, three separate customers told the detectives that they thought the murders might have been committed by a very jealous local thug who hung out at the bar and whose ex-wife had dated one of the victims. Although not married to her any longer, this man still became incensed whenever his ex-wife even talked to another man. The detectives looked into it, and given this man's reputation and police record, they realized he was certainly another possibility to consider.

The list of possible suspects just seemed to keep getting longer and longer. According to the *Indianapolis News*, the city's afternoon newspaper, by December 3, 1971, the police said they had three definite suspects they were looking at—but the truth was that they had many more possible suspects, and many, many people of interest yet to be interviewed. They hadn't even gotten to most of the women listed on the men's scorecard yet. The investigation seemed to grow more involved and complex with every person they talked to.

On December 4, 1971, the Grinsteiner Funeral Home in Indianapolis held the funerals for James Barker and

Robert Gierse, one right after the other. They held Bark-er's at 1:00 P.M. and Gierse's at 1:30 P.M. (On December 5, 1971, Joyner's Funeral Home in Wilson, North Carolina, held Robert Hinson's funeral.) The police naturally attended the ceremonies in Indianapolis, both to pay their respects and to see who attended. Through experience, the police knew that a killer will often come to a victim's funeral because he wants to hear what people are saying about the murder. Interestingly, of the eighty-five people present at the two funerals, officers reported that half of them were young, attractive women. Aside from that note, however, nothing else at the funerals seemed unusual.

Hinson's family buried him at the Evergreen Memorial Cemetery in Wilson, North Carolina; Gierse's family buried him at the Sts. Peter and Paul Cemetery in St. Louis, Missouri; and Barker's family buried him at the Odd Fellows Cemetery in Salem, West Virginia.

After attending the funerals, and as part of their investigation, the detectives then visited a large number of the kind of cheap taverns in Indianapolis that the victims were known to frequent. They hoped to pick up rumors of any threats made against the men or to find out about any other incidents that might lead someone to want to kill them. Alas, ultimately the detectives didn't learn much from the people at these taverns, but they did hear from several of those close to Bob Hinson that for the last month or so he had been very moody and depressed, not his usual happy, ready-to-party self. However, these people said, he had refused to talk about what was bothering him. The detectives naturally wondered if the source of Hinson's unhappiness could have had anything to do with the motive behind the murders. Did he know or suspect that someone intended to kill him?

On December 6, 1971, six days after the murders, detectives interviewed April Lynn Smoot, the woman whom Bob Gierse had sent $50 when she and her husband were stranded in New Orleans. When asked about the day of the murders, she said that she had driven by the office of B&B Microfilming that day and saw Gierse's and Hinson's cars parked there but didn't stop. She also told the detectives that she had talked to Hinson on the telephone the day of the murders at around 4:30 P.M. It had just been a friendly conversation, and there'd been no hint of anything bad about to happen. When asked about her husband, she shrugged and said that he had left her and she believed he was probably headed back to Louisiana. She told the detectives that her husband, David Lynn, had left town for New Orleans on December 1, 1971—the day the murders were discovered—which seemed very suspicious, since Lynn was reported to the police to be an extremely jealous man who had once allegedly beaten and threatened to kill her and others because he suspected she was involved with Gierse. When asked about her husband's whereabouts on the night of the murders, she gave Lynn an alibi for the entire night, saying that on the night of November 30, 1971, they and another couple had spent the evening going to several taverns. She said that she spent the whole night with her husband. However, she later became very upset when the detectives caught her in several lies concerning other events. The detectives, naturally suspicious, asked her if she would be willing to take a lie detector test, and she said she would. Ultimately, the test showed that she was telling the truth about her lack of participation in the crime. However, the test operator said that he had questions about whether or not she believed her husband might be involved.

The detectives then reinterviewed Louise Cole and Diane Horton, two women who had reportedly been sleeping with the victims, and who also had, respectively, a very jealous husband and ex-husband. However, they didn't get any new information of significance out of either woman. Detective Sergeant Michael Popcheff would later say that Diane Horton seemed to him to have been either a very unobservant or uninterested witness in many of the events the three victims had been involved in. She often traveled with the men when they went somewhere, but when asked by the detectives who the men met, what they discussed, or what the men did, she would always say she didn't know. She claimed she usually waited in the car, and apparently never asked the men about where they'd been or what they'd done.

Even though the detectives already had a long list of possible suspects, they soon began looking at the possibility of adding yet another one: Ted Uland. They had received reports that Records Security Corporation was experiencing serious financial difficulties and that this situation was getting only worse because B&B Microfilming had persuaded several important clients of Records Security Corporation to transfer their business to them. The detectives also discovered that Uland had taken out a $100,000 life insurance policy on Gierse and a $50,000 life insurance policy on Hinson, and that these policies were due to expire just a few weeks after the murders. This was a huge sum in 1971, and $150,000 for a company about to go under financially certainly seemed to give Uland the motive necessary for the murders.

However, as suspicious as those life insurance policies might have seemed on the surface, the detectives soon learned that taking out life insurance policies on key executives is a common practice in business. In addition, they found that Gierse had actually been the one to make payments through Records Security Corporation for these policies, and he'd also recently inquired about getting similar policies for himself and Hinson when they started up B&B Microfilming. This didn't appear to be some secret plot in a murder-for-profit scheme after all.

Nonetheless, the homicide detectives asked the Indiana State Police for any information they had in their files on Uland, who lived in Jasper, Indiana, about 125 miles south-southwest of Indianapolis. The state police reported back that Uland had no criminal record but was in significant monetary straits: The Cherokee Drilling Company, Uland's lead company, appeared to be in serious financial difficulty, and Uland was also in the process of being sued by an airplane company, a logging company, and an oil company.

Lieutenant Joe McAtee and his team also followed up on a tip that a man named Charles Blythe, the current general manager for Records Security Corporation, might have some knowledge about the crime. Blythe denied all knowledge of the murders, however, and passed a lie detector test. When asked by the detectives about the relationship between Gierse, Hinson, and Uland, Blythe said that as far as he knew they had all been friends, even after Gierse and Hinson had left to start their own company.

Interestingly, the state police investigator said that when he interviewed Uland's secretary, an Elizabeth Angle, she told him that she had recently accompanied Uland on a visit to the North LaSalle Street house. However, she also told him that she was "scared to death" to be working for Uland, and that she was terrified "they" would get her if they realized how much she knew about Uland and the microfilming company in Indianapolis. She added that Uland's employees in the drilling business were the meanest, toughest people around. Yet she either didn't have or wouldn't share any information with the investigator about what would make anyone want to kill her, or who specifically she was afraid of. Ultimately, while the detectives found Miss Angle's information interesting, they dismissed her interview, figuring her comments about the danger she was in had more to do with her watching too much television and seeing too many movies than any real threats.

By December 8, 1971, more than a week after the murders, McAtee and his team realized that they didn't seem to be going anywhere. Instead of dropping names off their suspect list, the more they investigated, the more suspects they added. Their attempts to approach the case by establishing a motive seemed equally blocked.

"The biggest problem in most homicides is finding a motive," said Popcheff. "In this case we had at least five possible motives."

The detectives found that the three victims had been in arguments and fights with dozens of people in the bars they prowled on Friday nights, and they'd also been sleeping with dozens of other men's wives and girlfriends. There were a number of people, both in the men's business and social lives, who felt that the men had done them wrong. Consequently, because of the victims' lifestyles, McAtee and his team found that the list of possible motives, just like the list of suspects, continued to grow. The *Indianapolis Star* said of the North LaSalle Street case that it wasn't three murders that lacked a motive, but rather that there were too many possible motives. The crime could have been motivated by jealousy, involving three likely possibilities: an enraged father, a jealous husband or boyfriend, or even jealousy stemming from B&B's incredible success. Or, the newspaper theorized, the motive could have been financial: Maybe the men had borrowed money from loan sharks and were unable to pay it back, or perhaps it was a message from the Mob, who was trying to muscle in on the microfilm business. Or the murders could have been motivated by revenge, coming from someone the trio had reportedly embarrassed or humiliated in one of the cheap bars they prowled. But which was it?

The detectives realized that, like narrowing their investigation in order to pinpoint a suspect, they needed to do the same with a motive. According to the coroner, the murderer or murderers had grabbed the victims by the hair, stretched their necks taut, and then sliced through skin, muscle, cartilage, and bone. The blood flow would have been tremendous. And whoever did this had to do it three times. This meant the killer or killers had to be extremely motivated.

However, through their investigation, the detectives did realize that it was very unlikely that such a crime could have been committed by an amateur. And the idea of several amateurs teaming up seemed unlikely. The lack of forced entry, and especially the manner in which the three men were bound, pointed to someone who knew what he was doing. Consequently, news reports after the murders said that several of the detectives involved in the investigation suspected that the murders were the work of hired killers.

On December 9, 1971, the *Indianapolis Star* put forth the theory that the three men had been killed by organized crime as a warning not to try to stop the Mob infiltration of the microfilming business. Microfilming was relatively new technology but had the potential for making a lot of money. The newspaper also suggested the possibility that B&B Microfilming might have been just a front for the Mob, who had paid to start it up, or that perhaps the Mob had tried to muscle in on B&B and the men had resisted. This theory was supported by an earlier interview with Captain R. Wayne Hall, head of the Indiana State Police Organized Crime Unit, who, when asked if he thought it was possible that organized crime was involved in the North LaSalle Street murders, told the reporter, "You can read between the lines."

In addition to all of this, the possibility of loan sharks or some illegal source of money also arose. "These guys were spending money they weren't making," said Popcheff. "And we couldn't understand where that money was coming from." During their investigation, the detectives found that the men were spending a lot of money partying and drinking. Also, experts had told the detectives that starting up a business like B&B Microfilming would be an expensive venture, yet neither Gierse nor Hinson seemed to have the legitimate funds to do this. As a part of their investigation, the detectives obtained copies of tax returns for Gierse and Hinson and found that their expenses far outweighed their income. Where had the extra money come from? Was it a motive for the murders?

The possible motives in the case, like the list of suspects, seemed to just keep multiplying. An article appeared in the *Indianapolis News* on December 9, 1971, claiming that the police had established a definite motive in the case, but this was only an attempt by the police to

unnerve the murderer in the hopes that he would consequently make a mistake. In truth, the police still had
many motives and many suspects.

Meanwhile, on December 7, 1971, the detectives had
returned once more to the North LaSalle Street neighborhood to try to talk with neighbors they'd previously
been unable to contact. They finally found and interviewed a neighbor who said she had seen something suspicious on the night of the murders: a yellow car with
three men sitting in it parked across the street from 1318,
which she said sat there for several hours. She had never
seen this car or its occupants in the neighborhood before. The detectives knew this information could be crucial and that they would now need to interview every
single person on the block to see if anyone else had seen
the car or the men in it.

On December 8, 1971, McAtee and his team were
still no closer to solving the case when they received a
report from an Indianapolis police officer who said he
had talked with a man named Ron Lisby, an employee
of a company called Scott Graphics on East 52nd Street
in Indianapolis. Lisby, as it turned out, had helped Gierse
and Hinson get several of the very lucrative contracts
they had at B&B Microfilming and had loaned them
some equipment to use at their new business. But much
more importantly, he told the officer that he had once visited Gierse and Hinson at their home, where he claimed
he met a motorcycle bum who was apparently a friend
of Gierse and Hinson's, and reportedly on parole for

manslaughter. Lisby said he later learned that the man stole a motorcycle and $1,000 from Gierse and Hinson, and that Gierse had supposedly sworn out a warrant for him. The parolee only had one eye, Lisby said, and claimed that he lost the other one in a knife fight. The detectives reluctantly added another person to their list of suspects.

The police officer, while at Scott Graphics, also spoke with a man named Lafayette Robert Roe. Roe told the officer that he'd had his car, a 1964 cream-colored Chevrolet Impala, stolen from the rear of Scott Graphics just before the triple murder. He said that Marion County sheriff's deputies had recovered his car on December 1, 1971, in the 2000 block of South Ritter Avenue, a little over four miles to the south of the North LaSalle Street address. Upon reclaiming his car, Roe said that he found red stains on the rear seat, floor, and inside of the right door. It looked to him like blood, as if someone sitting there had been bleeding. The detectives, upon receiving this information, sent a crime lab technician out to check the stains, which the technician indeed found to test positive for type O human blood. All of the victims on North LaSalle Street, however, had been blood type A. Still, the detectives wondered, could the type O blood be the killer's? Could the murderer have possibly cut himself in all of the slashing and left some of his own blood behind?

On December 9, 1971, while still trying to retrace the victims' movements in the days just before the murders, a detective took a statement from Sandra Ann Hannemann, a woman who told them that she had met Barker, Gierse, and Hinson at the Sherman Bar on November 26, 1971. She met them, she said, when Barker came over and asked her to dance. On the night of the murders, between 7:00 and 8:00 P.M., the woman told the detectives, she had received a telephone call from Barker inquiring about a date they had set up that night at the Sherman Bar. He told her that he was calling from Gierse's house on North LaSalle Street. She said that the conversation lasted only about ten minutes and that she didn't hear any noise in the background, as though he was there at the house by himself.

For more than a week now, even though detectives had worked intensely, the investigation didn't seem to be going anywhere—but then suddenly a potentially crucial piece of information turned up. The detectives discovered that Jim Barker's previous address had been burglarized the night before the murders. Had the killer believed that Barker still lived there and hoped to catch him alone? The detectives realized that if the burglary detective could come up with some suspects in that case, it could provide a huge break in their investigation, too. But they also knew they couldn't just wait on that. It might happen. It might not. They had to keep their own investigation going.

While in the little over a week they had been assigned to the North LaSalle Street murders the detectives had conducted dozens of interviews, they'd also had to spend a lot of time wading through and examining all of the evidence from the murders. And there was plenty. Crime lab technicians had taken a large number of fingerprints from the house and the victims' cars. They had recovered fingerprints from beer and whiskey bottles, drinking glasses, door moldings, and a telephone. They also found a good fingerprint on an ashtray but discovered that it belonged to Diane Horton, Gierse's girlfriend. Likewise, James T. Cole's fingerprints on the inside glass of the front door were easily explained away because he had attended several parties at the house. The fact that so many people, including a number of the suspects, had been in and out of the North LaSalle Street house while attending one of the many parties held there meant that most of these fingerprints, like the ones found of Horton and Cole, didn't prove to be of much value.

In addition, the crime lab personnel and the coroner had taken many other items as evidence, including the clothing the men wore, hair samples, fingernail scrapings, a bloody pillow found on the floor, many blood samples from throughout the house, and even pieces of the tile floor, but again, though the detectives had been hopeful, these items didn't point toward any specific suspect. The detectives also hadn't been able to find a suspect with boots or overshoes matching the diamond design left in the hallway.

During their investigation, the detectives had, naturally, also gone to the offices of B&B Microfilming on East 10th Street. There they took as evidence a considerable amount of paperwork, in the hopes that it might alert them to someone with a serious grudge against the men. But again, though the detectives spent many hours going through the stack of papers, no definite suspect turned up.

However, something crucial to the case did appear at the offices of B&B Microfilming (adding another layer of complexity to a case that was already unbelievably complex). While there, the detectives discovered that a piece of equipment present—a typewriter used by B&B—had previously been reported to the police as stolen. And as they investigated further, the detectives found that this wasn't the only piece of suspicious equipment there. Detectives discovered that Gierse had reported a burglary at Records Security Corporation on June 25, 1969, in which $5,500 in microfilming equipment had been stolen. The police officer sent to take the report, however, had felt that the report was very questionable. Not only had there been no signs of forced entry, but only certain pieces of equipment had been taken, while other equally valuable pieces had been left behind. The detective assigned to the case additionally said in his report that he was told conflicting stories about the missing equipment and that he had learned Records Security Corporation was experiencing serious financial difficulties at that time. The detective suspected it might be an insurance scam.

However, although all signs pointed to a scam, it apparently wasn't for the insurance. The detectives investigating the North LaSalle Street murders found that while much of the equipment at B&B Microfilming had had their serial numbers removed, the items appeared identical to the equipment listed as stolen in the burglary reported by Gierse. On December 9, 1971, the police department had eighteen pieces of microfilming equipment sent to the police property room to hold as evidence. Experts had told the detectives that it would take at least $10,000 to start up an operation like B&B Microfilming. The detectives had naturally wondered where this money had come from. The stolen equipment answered part of this question.

The detectives, because of the discovery of stolen property at B&B Microfilming, suddenly saw a possible new direction in the case. They began looking for a connection between the killings of John Terhorst, the murdered man who'd known the three men on North LaSalle Street, and that of a local burglar named Bobby Lee Atkinson, who had been murdered in a manner very similar to Terhorst: shot twice in the head and dumped in a lover's lane south of Indianapolis. Also, the detectives had discovered during their interviews that several witnesses to Gierse's ex-girlfriend Ilene Combest's tirade over another woman said that during it she had screamed she would expose Gierse's and Hinson's involvement in the "Vette deal." The police wondered if the three men had been murdered because they knew who Terhorst's killer was. Alas, however, although it was a good possibility, this new direction also went nowhere. The detectives could never turn up a connection.

In their search for a motive and suspect, the police

department hired the accounting firm of Geo. S. Olive & Co. to conduct a financial audit of B&B Microfilming to see if any clues could come from this. B&B Microfilming, the detectives learned, had not yet filed incorporation papers with the state, but had opened its bank accounts on September 17, 1971. The audit, however, didn't find anything other than a new business starting out with very limited funds.

Yet, the list of customers B&B Microfilming had attracted in its very brief life was nothing short of impressive. They had as customers a number of Indianapolis's biggest companies: Indiana National Bank, American Fletcher National Bank, and Merchants Bank (the three largest banks in Indianapolis at the time). In addition, they also held microfilming contracts with Pioneer Title Company, Anacomp, Blue Cross Blue Shield, the Federal Home Loan Bank, the Board of School Commissioners, and even the city government of Indianapolis itself.

The detectives were puzzled as to how such a new company, only a couple of months old, could have landed so many big contracts right away. This unusual success added yet another possible motive to the case. In 1971, big money could be made in the microfilming business. Could the murders have been committed by someone upset over how much of this money B&B Microfilming was getting? Had B&B Microfilming angered someone in the microfilming business by taking all of these big, and very profitable, customers?

The detectives had also learned that, even with the stolen equipment, B&B Microfilming would still have been very expensive to start up initially (renting office space, buying supplies, and so forth). Hinson, as far as the auditors could tell, had made no financial contribution at all to B&B Microfilming, and Gierse certainly couldn't have provided all of the money from his income. Could there have been silent partners? Or some other unknown source of income?

By December 12, 1971, almost two weeks after the murders had been discovered, most of the detectives assigned to the investigation, though not any closer to solving the case, had put in over three hundred hours of overtime without a day off. The detectives had already interviewed over six hundred people, and had many more people left to be interviewed. As might be imagined, numerous theories had been proposed during these interviews, from jealousy to the Mob, and from envious business concerns to the men's involvement in secret documents.

The local news media had also presented a number of theories. The *Indianapolis Star*, for example, put forth the idea that the killer or killers had only been after one of the men, and that the others had just gotten caught up in it. Many of the people who subscribed to this theory believed that the target was most likely Hinson. Witnesses had said that he had seemed very worried about something lately. Also, he was the one who had gotten into most of the fights.

The North LaSalle Street investigation, along with the problem of a large number of suspects and motives,

also suddenly ran into another serious handicap. Lieutenant McAtee reported this problem in a memo to his
captain and deputy chief on December 12, 1971. He said
that several of the people they interviewed, whose names
the news media printed, had, like the Cole family, begun
receiving threatening telephone calls. Because of this,
potential witnesses had become reluctant to talk to the
police.

Those who didn't live during the 1960s and '70s
might find it strange that individuals unrelated to the
case would call and threaten someone who had talked
to the police about what appeared to be the murder of
three men who didn't deserve the death they received.
But during this time period, because of the civil rights
and antiwar movements in the United States, many people looked unfavorably upon the police, seeing them as
an occupying army whose purpose was to suppress the
rights of those involved in or supporting those movements. Consequently, during this time, anyone cooperat-
ing with the police was seen by many people as conspiring
with the enemy.

Despite these difficulties, and while they hadn't made
a lot of progress in the previous two weeks, the detectives
were not even close to giving up yet. They had already
talked to several of the women on the men's scorecard.
However, because this list contained only first names (or
in some cases, just nicknames), the detectives were having some serious problems finding many of these women.
Also, a lot of the women had apparently been one-night
stands, and so friends of the three victims couldn't help

the police identify them. The detectives realized, though, that a solution to the case could come from any name on this list. And so, the detectives knew they couldn't give up. They had to find as many of these women as they could.

CHAPTER FOUR

On December 13, 1971, Captain Raymond Koers, head of the Indianapolis Police Department Homicide Branch, said to reporters, "I am confident we will make an arrest, or arrests, in this case."

This statement, of course, was meant to reassure the public that the police were on the job, and that there was no reason for them to fear becoming the next victim of the North LaSalle Street murderer. However, despite Captain Koers's public optimism about solving the North LaSalle Street case, it didn't reassure those actually working on the investigation. The detectives assigned to the case were still putting in long hours without any solution in sight. Deputy Chief of Investigations Ralph Lumpkin was considering assigning additional detectives to the investigation because the original detectives would often work twenty to twenty-four hours straight on the case.

"Because we didn't have a solid motive, this became a really tough case to solve," said Detective Sergeant Michael Popcheff. "We worked around the clock on it. We were going home, laying down for a couple of hours, and then coming back to work. It was that intense. I even missed my sister's wedding because of it."

After two weeks of questioning witnesses and suspects, of examining evidence, of chasing down one false lead after another, and of continuously turning up more and more suspects rather than eliminating them, the original exhilaration and certainty of solution had begun to fade. Still, the detectives hadn't given up the hope of solving the triple murder. No one thought it was unsolvable; it was just much tougher than they had anticipated. This case had turned out to be much more complex and difficult than it had appeared to be at the murder scene. The detectives assigned to the case knew that they simply needed to find that one witness or one piece of evidence that would lead them to the right suspect. None of the detectives doubted that such a witness or piece of evidence existed. It was there. They just hadn't found it yet.

At the start of the third week of the investigation, the detectives finally did manage to narrow the investigation a bit. McAtee and his team told reporters that they felt they had at least eliminated the possibility of a connection between the North LaSalle Street murders and the murders of John Terhorst and Bobby Atkinson. Although the police had looked into the possibilities that Atkinson had sold some stolen equipment to Gierse and Hinson when they started up B&B Microfilming, that

Atkinson and Terhorst had been murdered by the same person, and that the victims on North LaSalle Street had had some knowledge about the Terhorst and Atkinson murders, they hadn't turned up any evidence to support any of these theories.

The detectives talked to a friend of the three victims who told them that he had stopped by the North LaSalle Street house on Sunday morning, November 28, and was met at the door by Hinson, who handed him a glass of scotch. The man said that when he walked inside the house he encountered two women in the living room with two children in tow, and that the women were making a scene. He said he didn't know why, but the women were extremely angry and upset about something. In the bathroom, the man went on, Gierse sat in the tub while a woman in her bra and panties scrubbed his back. Gierse and the woman had paid no attention to the commotion in the living room. Although the police questioned many friends and acquaintances of the victims, they were never able to identify or locate the two angry women.

The detectives also learned from witnesses that at around 8:00 P.M. on the same Sunday, a woman had pulled up to 1318 North LaSalle Street in a yellow Oldsmobile, got out, and pounded on the front door. The witnesses said that the woman was crying profusely. Even though Gierse's and Hinson's cars sat parked on the street in front of the house, no one answered the door. The woman, still crying, finally stormed off of the porch and went back and sat in her car. Concerned neighbors called the police, who came and spoke with the woman. She told the officers that she was all right, that she had just had a fight with her boyfriend was all. She didn't say which of the men on North LaSalle Street was presumably her boyfriend. The officers, who dealt with many such minor domestic disputes every day, sent her on her way but didn't think enough of the incident to take down her name. Though they later searched, the detectives were never able to locate this woman.

On December 15, 1971, Detective Sergeant Pat Stark, still assisting in the North LaSalle Street investigation, traveled to Chicago to conduct a background investigation on the three slaying victims. Sometimes murders can be committed by individuals who were wronged a long time ago, and who have let their emotions boil and fester until they finally burst open into rage. Detective Sergeant Stark hoped to find some evidence of this, and if not, at least some evidence that could give a direction to the investigation.

Sergeant Stark met with the Chicago chief of detectives and the homicide commander but found that the Chicago Police Department had no record of the three men ever being arrested or involved in any major investigation by the police department there. Next, Stark drove to the office where all three victims had been employed before coming to Indianapolis. Stark talked with several men who had been Gierse's, Hinson's, and Barker's immediate supervisors, and all of them said that they had only known the victims through their work at the plant and had never gone out socially with them. All of the supervisors said that the three men were very hard workers who had seemed to want to learn all they could about the microfilming business. All of the supervisors Stark talked to agreed, however, that of the three men, Barker seemed to be the one with a temper problem. They said he could get angry very easily.

When he checked the men's personnel files, Stark found that Gierse and Hinson had left Bell and Howell employment on good terms and were eligible for rehire. Several of the people there told Stark that Gierse and Hinson returned to the plant for a visit whenever they were in Chicago. The two men would tell their former fellow employees how well they were doing in the microfilming business in Indianapolis, and how much better they expected it to be in the future. Barker, at the time of his death, had still been employed by Bell and Howell, in Indianapolis.

Since James Barker's ex-wife, Paula Palmer, still lived in Chicago, Stark thought it would be a good idea to pay her a visit. Among the best sources on a man's background, the detective knew, were ex-wives. Most exes feel no need to protect the man's reputation and will often tell police secrets they certainly wouldn't have shared if they were still married. Stark knew that if there was any dirt to be had on Barker's life in Chicago, his ex-wife would know and would probably be willing to talk about it. Many, many crimes have been solved by talking to ex-wives.

Chicago Police detective Robert Friedman accompanied Stark to visit Barker's ex-wife (a common courtesy police departments typically extend to officers from other jurisdictions investigating a crime). Paula Palmer told the two detectives that she and Jim Barker had been married from December 1966 to February 1970. She said that they'd often had disagreements because he had never been satisfied with what they had, but had always wanted something better, even if they couldn't afford it. She also told the detectives that, despite this desire to have better things, Barker would never take her to nice places when they went out, but had instead preferred "hillbilly taverns," where, she said, he could feel that he was better than everyone else. There had been some serious insecurities in his personality.

She also told Stark and Friedman something startling and unexpected, considering the sexual conquest scorecard the detectives had found in the North LaSalle Street house, and particularly since Barker had held the lead in the contest: She said that Barker hadn't seemed interested in having sex with her. Paula Palmer told the detectives that she discovered Barker would rather read pornography and masturbate than have sex with her, even though she said she tried to get him to have sex on numerous occasions. She told them that she had tried everything, including wearing sexy nightwear, but that he would tell her "to get the hell away from him." In his report, Stark, apparently puzzled by this revelation, added the comment: "Mrs. Barker was not an ugly woman!"

Palmer then added that her ex-husband had had a really bad temper and was not afraid of confrontation, and that he had always wanted to start a fight with anyone he felt had offended him. He wouldn't be afraid, she said, to jump out of the car and run over and punch a driver who'd done something to irritate him. She also said that he liked to be obnoxious and a smart aleck. He seemed, for some reason, to enjoy offending people. Stark could begin to see part of the reason the three men had been involved in so many bar fights.

Paula Palmer said that, as the detectives might imagine, their marriage had not been a happy one, and that she had tried unsuccessfully to get Barker to go to counseling. She said, however, that after he beat her several times, she filed for divorce. She told the detectives that the last time she had spoken with Barker was by telephone on October 27, 1971, when he told her that Bell and Howell was going to cut his salary and so he was thinking about leaving them and going into business with Gierse and Hinson at B&B Microfilming. She also added that whenever she saw Barker and Gierse together, her ex seemed very jealous of Gierse's clothing and car. Before the detectives left, Paula gave Sergeant Stark a stack of letters that Barker had written her, in the hopes they might contain something of value to the case. Sergeant Stark thanked her but knew he was returning to Indianapolis without much new information that would help in the investigation. While Palmer had given the officers all of the dirt she knew about her ex-husband, none of it had really assisted in the search for the murderer.

On December 19, 1971, almost three weeks after the murders, Lieutenant Joe McAtee and Detective Sergeants Mike Popcheff and Jim Strode submitted a thirty-eight-page progress report on the North LaSalle Street case. In

the report they requested approval to add two more detectives full-time to the investigative team. Detective Sergeants Pat Stark and Bob Tirmenstein had been assisting
part-time, but now, upon approval, would work full-time
to help the three already full-time detectives assigned to
the case. What McAtee, Popcheff, and Strode didn't say,
but was implied by this request, was that what had looked
like a case that would close quickly had turned out to be
anything but.

As a part of their progress report, the detectives told
of how a uniformed street lieutenant had called the Homicide Office and advised them that he had learned the
SupeRx Drug Store a half block from B&B Microfilming
on East 10th Street had developed some photographs
that had apparently been taken at Bob Gierse's birthday
party on November 18. The lieutenant also learned that
Wava Winslow, one of Jim Barker's girlfriends, had come
into the store and tried to pay for and pick up the photographs. The manager of the store, however, knowing
about the police investigation of the triple murder, had
put her off and managed to snap a Polaroid picture of
her before she left. The detectives instructed the lieutenant to get the photographs and bring them to the Homicide Office. They hoped that the photographs might
show someone at the party they weren't aware of. However, though they studied the photographs intently, nothing of significance came of this lead.

The report also talked about the detectives' attempts
to locate the women on the three men's sexual conquest
scorecard, and about how they weren't having much

success. A lot of these women, the detectives found, had apparently been one-night stands picked up in bars, and so the people who knew the victims didn't know them, which made locating these women very difficult. In addition, the three men apparently had nicknames for some of the women that they had shared only among themselves.

The detectives, in their report, also told about contacting the Homicide Branch of the St. Louis Police Department. McAtee and his team had received information from several witnesses that the three victims had been arrested while attending a football game there in November of 1971. Perhaps, the detectives thought, the men had gotten into a dispute with someone who could be considered a suspect. The detectives in St. Louis said that they would look into it and send any reports they could find.

The progress report then went on to tell of a message the detectives had received from the St. Johns County Sheriff's Office in Florida. It stated that a man in custody there had claimed to be the one who had committed the triple murder in Indianapolis. The man had no identification on him and his identity had not yet been learned. Upon calling the department in Florida, the detectives spoke with a deputy there who told them that they had arrested a very shabbily dressed man of Puerto Rican descent who told them that he had committed the triple murder in Indianapolis. The deputy said that the man told them this in English and then began speaking Spanish and hadn't spoken English since. It was believed that the man had serious mental problems, however, and the deputy told the detectives that the triple murder case in Indianapolis had been on the news in Florida, so the man might have learned about it that way. Although the Indianapolis detectives didn't consider the man a viable suspect, they requested that the St. Johns County Sheriff's Office send Indianapolis whatever information they could obtain about him.

Strange as it might seem, false confession is not an uncommon occurrence in murder cases that garner a lot of publicity. Often, individuals with serious mental problems want to confess to these crimes, causing major problems for investigators. Whether it is because these individuals have deluded themselves into believing they actually did commit the crime, or because they feel they deserve to be punished for some other misdeed, and confessing to the crime is how they do it, it is often hard to determine. Many of these individuals have also read up on and studied the case, so they seem to have an intimate knowledge of it, just as a real suspect would. Such false confessions are part of why homicide detectives never release all of the details of a major crime to the public. Mentally disturbed individuals who want to confess to a crime, though they may be thoroughly versed in the case, will not know these undisclosed details.

In their progress report, the detectives went on to tell of visiting restaurants and taverns the men frequented. At the White Front Tavern, they learned from customers of yet another person of interest in the case, a regular who might have had a motive for the murders. One of the victims had dated his wife. The detectives took all of the information they could get about the man and then asked the owner of the bar to notify them when the man came in. They didn't say it in their report, but one thing the detectives certainly didn't need was another suspect.

But the suspects kept coming. In an interview with Carol Ann Faulkner, a former girlfriend of Jim Barker's, the detectives became apprised of yet another person whom the three men had made very angry. She told them that after she and Barker started dating, one time she, Barker, and Hinson had gone with a friend of theirs named Dick Roller and his girlfriend to a tavern. Barker and Hinson had persuaded Roller's girlfriend to get up onstage and sing a song, but once she did, they began making fun of her. Incensed, Roller grabbed his girlfriend and stormed out of the tavern.

Further investigation into this incident with Roller and his girlfriend brought the detectives in contact with a lady named Sharon Mitchell, who said that she and Roller had moved to Indianapolis together from Dallas, that Jim Barker had moved in with them for a while—and that when Roller found a new girlfriend, she moved out and started dating Barker. To add more complicated connections, Mitchell also told the detectives that she was now living with Ilene Combest, Gierse's old girlfriend.

Although Mitchell mentioned that Roller had moved back to Texas prior to the murders, which was later confirmed (and so wasn't a suspect), detectives would learn that the manner in which the three victims had treated

Roller's girlfriend wasn't an isolated case—the three men had seemed to really enjoy embarrassing or humiliating people. Witnesses also said that the men liked to bully and try to intimidate people. This information, the detectives knew, only added the possibility of many more suspects. Someone who'd been deeply embarrassed or humiliated in public might have felt motivated to kill, even in as vicious a manner as had been done on North LaSalle Street.

The report also mentioned yet another couple of wrinkles in the case. The detectives interviewed a man named Bob McAbe, a business associate of Bob Gierse's who worked for the 3M Corporation. McAbe told the detectives that he and Gierse would help each other with business leads, and that Gierse had tried to persuade him to quit 3M and come work for him. On the morning of November 30, 1971, McAbe said, he had spoken with Gierse on the telephone and Gierse had asked him if he had ever worked with classified material. McAbe said he had. "Isn't that [a] hell of a way to do business," Gierse had responded. The detectives had also heard from other sources that the men were working with secret material, yet the records of B&B Microfilming didn't show any contracts with organizations that might want classified material microfilmed. Had Gierse just been trying to make it seem as if they did?

The detectives had wanted to conduct a follow-up interview with Diane Horton, Gierse's girlfriend, but hadn't been able to reach her by telephone. Consequently, the detectives sent a police car out to check the security of her residence since, like many of those involved in the case, she had earlier reported receiving threatening telephone calls. The officer didn't find anything amiss there, and the detectives were finally able to contact Diane and have her come into the Homicide Office. They also had Louise Cole and April Lynn Smoot return for more questioning.

They learned from these interviews that Gierse and Hinson had gone to the Big Wheel Restaurant in Bloomington, Indiana, in late September to meet with Ted Uland, just two days after Hinson had left the company. The two men were accompanied to the meeting by Gierse's on-and-off girlfriend, Ilene Combest. Reportedly, after a few minutes, when Hinson had said that he wouldn't change his mind about leaving Records Security Corporation, Uland had excused him, and Hinson went out and sat in the car with Combest. Gierse and Uland then talked for almost two hours. The detectives made a note to follow up with Ilene Combest and see if they could find out what Gierse and Uland had talked about.

Later in their report, the detectives mentioned speaking with a Mrs. King, who also lived on North La-Salle Street. In addition to corroborating that streams of young women would come and go at all hours from Gierse and Hinson's house, Mrs. King also stated that on the night of November 30, 1971, she had seen an unfamiliar light-colored car parked in front of their place. She had never seen the car in the neighborhood before. She told the detectives that she saw the car there at between 9:30 and 10:00 P.M.

In addition to Mrs. King and the neighbor interviewed on December 7, the detectives then found a third
person in the neighborhood who had witnessed the same
car parked there. He also said he'd never seen the car in
the area before and had walked by it, noticing that the
license plate had a 26A prefix (meaning that it came
from Gibson County in southern Indiana). While this
should have raised red flags for the detectives investigating the murders, it didn't. This license plate is mentioned
in the progress report but nowhere else in the homicide
case file. For some unknown reason, the detectives didn't
appear to follow up on this information about the unusual license plate or attempt to find the owner of this
car, or if they did, they didn't generate any paperwork
about their efforts.

The detectives would, however, eventually talk to a
fourth witness about this mystery car. "About two weeks
after the murders we hear from a witness that a car with
three guys in it was sitting across the street from the
murder scene," said Detective Sergeant Popcheff.

In mid-December, another neighbor on North La-
Salle, Michael Ray, told the police that on the night of
the murders, he'd been walking home from his brother's
house on North Kealing Avenue, five blocks east, and had
walked along the 1300 block of North LaSalle Street.
On that night, he said, he saw a light-colored dirty car
with three males sitting in it, parked across the street
from the house. He said that the driver had looked
strangely at him as he passed by, and that as he kept
walking he noticed a man sitting in the backseat also

watching him. He gave the police a very general description of the men, saying the man in the backseat looked about thirty to thirty-one, and was heavyset, with a round face, black hair, and bushy sideburns. The one in the front seat, he said, appeared older and slimmer. He told the police he didn't see what the third man looked like.

"They were drinking beer and throwing their bottles out onto the ground. But by the time we found out it was too late," lamented Popcheff years later. The detectives knew that the beer bottles would have contained fingerprints that could have been key pieces of evidence. Popcheff said they asked the man why, since he knew there had been a triple murder, he hadn't called the police earlier. Ray replied that he'd been busy with school and just hadn't gotten around to it.

Popcheff would later say that incidents like that seemed to plague the North LaSalle Street investigation. It was a case, he said, that the detectives just couldn't seem to ever get a grip on.

The report then told of an additional development in the case that raised the possibility of yet another suspect in the ever-increasing pool. Working on a tip, the detectives went to the Merry-Go-Round Bar on East New York Street and spoke with the bartender, who told them that a man named Phil Pickard had been in the tavern the previous night, bragging about how good he was with a knife and how he had killed three men with one. The bartender said that Pickard had been so drunk that he had personally driven him home. The detectives went to Mr. Pickard's residence and picked him up, taking him down to the Homicide Office, where they questioned him.

Pickard said that he remembered the bartender taking him home, but denied any knowledge of the North LaSalle Street murders. The detectives showed Pickard some crime scene photos to see his reaction, but he showed no signs of being upset. When asked if he would take a lie detector test, he agreed to.

Pickard was just one of several individuals throughout the course of the investigation who would falsely brag that they had a connection to the murders. It's not an uncommon phenomenon in highly publicized crimes—men will often want to impress or scare others, and so they will brag or hint that they committed some infamous crime. With just a little investigation, though, the police could usually dismiss these claims for the empty boasts they were.

In their progress report the detectives also told of how, in response to a tip, they went to the Marion County Recorder's Office to check on a report that the federal government had put a lien against Records Security Corporation. The detectives had been told by several people that Records Security Corporation was in serious financial straits, and they found that indeed, on December 2, 1971, the federal government had put a lien of $6,385.88 for back taxes against Records Security Corporation. The detectives also learned that this wasn't the first time; it turned out that the federal government had put several other liens against the business in the past.

On December 11, 1971, the report said, the homicide detectives had Ted Uland come into the Homicide Office for an interview. He brought with him some records that the detectives had requested from Records Security Corporation. They advised Uland of his constitutional rights against self-incrimination. He said he understood them, but then refused to sign the waiver of rights form, although he agreed to talk with the detectives.

Uland told them that the insurance policies on Gierse and Hinson had been taken out by Gierse, not him, and that he'd recently found out that they were in effect only until December 10, 1971. In any case, he added, some question had apparently arisen as to whether or not the insurance company would pay off because neither man worked for the company any longer.

When asked about the meeting with Gierse and Hinson in Bloomington, Uland said that it had occurred on September 26, 1971, and that he had offered Hinson $5,000 to stay with Records Security Corporation until the end of the year. He had really needed him. Hinson, however, had refused. Uland then told the detectives that for some reason Hinson had brought a gun along with him to the meeting, though Uland was unable to describe or give any other information about the gun. The detectives still listed Uland as a possible suspect, and when they offered him two dates for a lie detector test, he wouldn't commit, but said that he would have to get back to them.

As a part of the investigation, the detectives also brought in a certified public accountant and asked him to look through the Records Security Corporation paperwork given to them by Uland. In this paperwork, the accountant found what he believed to be at least nine forged checks drawn up and signed by Gierse in amounts from $30 to $140. When contacted by the detectives, the men these checks had been made out to stated that they hadn't seen the checks or endorsed them. This piqued the interest of the detectives, who'd heard from several sources that Gierse might have been stealing money from Records Security Corporation.

Was this, they wondered, how Gierse had financed his lifestyle and new business start-up? By stealing money and equipment from his former employer? The incident Louise Cole had spoken about, in which Gierse suspected that Uland had come into the house on North LaSalle Street to take canceled checks, suddenly took on new relevance. Had Uland, the detectives also wondered, suspected or known that Gierse was writing phony checks and wanted evidence? This, if true, would certainly move Uland up on the suspect list, particularly since he hadn't mentioned anything about the checks to the detectives.

The detectives then talked with a Sharon Bidwell, who worked at the Executive Health Club in downtown Indianapolis and had dated Jim Barker. The three victims had all been members of the club. She told them that when Gierse and Hinson formed B&B Microfilming, Barker had acquired an expensive piece of microfilming equipment and gave it to them. Bidwell didn't know how Barker had come to obtain this piece of equipment. The detectives found this particularly interesting because, of the three men, Barker seemed to have had the most money problems. Bidwell also mentioned in passing that Bob Hinson had once dated a married WAC (Women's Army Corps) officer from nearby Fort Harrison, who might be on the men's scorecard.

Hinson seemed to have had no problem dating married women—the report also tells of a police officer who brought his sister-in-law, who had dated Hinson for several weeks, into the Homicide Office. Even though she was married, she said she didn't think dating Hinson had bothered her husband because she had dated other men in the past and he hadn't been upset about it then.

Bob Hinson's own ex-wife, Geraldine Hinson, wasn't much help, either. She told detectives that she and Hinson had been married for six years and were on good terms, visiting each other often. She did say that Hinson always seemed to be short of money.

Another witness the detectives spoke to, the owner of a liquor store, also said he'd heard that Gierse and Hinson had swindled Uland out of some money—though he also brought up the possibility of Gierse and Hinson being involved in industrial spying or spying on the government agencies whose documents they microfilmed. (He admitted to detectives, however, that he had no proof or evidence of any of this. It was only what he had heard or suspected.)

The detectives told in their report of having gone to the Idle Hour Tavern in Indianapolis to speak with another one of Hinson's girlfriends, a Norma Jean Duran, who threw a further complication into the case. She told the detectives that a male friend of Barker's had dated a female FBI employee who would sometimes get information on people for Barker. Duran didn't know who Barker wanted information on or what he needed the information for, but she said that the three men had told her several times that they had been involved with some kind of syndicate while living in Chicago, and that they had to be very careful. Was this the truth or just empty boasting that the men hoped would impress young ladies, particularly young ladies at the type of taverns they frequented? The detectives didn't really know.

In the course of their investigation, the detectives also learned that April Lynn Smoot's husband had moved back to Indianapolis from New Orleans, and that he and his wife were now living together. When called, April's husband, David Lynn, said that he didn't feel like coming into the Homicide Office right then. Detectives went out and picked him up. At that moment, considering his reported level of jealousy—and the fact that he'd left town on the day the murders had been discovered—David Lynn still stood high on the suspect list. The detectives questioned him extensively but couldn't find any serious inconsistencies in his story. When asked, he voluntarily took a lie detector test and passed it. The detectives ultimately eliminated him as a suspect.

Adding another bit of good news, the detectives said

in their report that they felt they could also eliminate another one of their key suspects: Louise Cole's husband, James T. Cole, who had come into the office and taken a lie detector test, which showed that he had no knowledge of the crime. At last, the detectives thought, the case was moving forward. With Mr. Lynn and Mr. Cole removed, the detectives felt that they were finally eliminating from, rather than adding to, the suspect list.

The detectives ended their report with the comment that they had interviewed many people not talked about in the report but hadn't mentioned them because these individuals didn't contribute anything to the case. They also said that they had many more people yet to interview. The case was still very much open.

After three weeks, the detectives realized that, even with all of the work they'd done so far, they hadn't found the kind of evidence yet that could point them toward any one suspect. While they had finally eliminated several key suspects, many possible ones still remained. But no one suspect stood out as more likely than the others. The detectives knew that they needed to find some more physical evidence that could tie one person to the case.

And so, on December 20, 1971, the Indianapolis Police Department sent the bedsheets, pillowcases, and cloth strips used to tie and gag the men to the FBI Laboratory in Washington, D.C. (In the early 1970s local police departments seldom had the laboratory facilities to do much more than rudimentary science. If extensive scientific testing needed to be done, the materials were often sent to the FBI Crime Laboratory.) The Indianapolis Police wanted the federal investigators to see if they could recover any fingerprints from the fabric, and also asked the FBI to have a study done on the knots used to tie the cords around two of the victims' hands. The knots had appeared unusual, and the detectives hoped they might be able to provide a clue.

Unfortunately, on January 19, 1972, the police department received notice from the FBI that they couldn't recover any usable fingerprints from the materials sent and didn't have any information about the knots. Another dead end.

And as if McAtee and his team didn't already have enough wrinkles in the case, the detectives, when talking to people who knew the three men or knew people who knew them, began picking up rumors that the three victims might have been killed because they'd been involved in pornography trafficking. In the 1970s, long before the advent of the Internet, pornography was circulated in printed or film form. Because pornography was illegal in many communities, pornographic photos, magazines, movies, and books were often distributed much like drugs were, through criminal networks. Dealing with these networks, like dealing with drug cartels, could be dangerous, so these tips struck the detectives as worth checking out.

One of the people who had given the police this information about pornography trafficking was Elwood Rogers, a man who'd done microfilm business with Gierse.

He told the police that a couple of years before the murders, Gierse had given him the telephone number of a man who lived in Avon, Indiana, and who was supposedly involved in pornography. Rogers said that he believed Gierse and this man might have been partners in trafficking pornography. Like dealing in drugs, dealing in pornography in the early 1970s could be very profitable. The detectives wondered if this was how Gierse and Hinson had gotten the money to start up B&B Microfilming.

Rogers told the detectives that he knew about the sex contest and that Gierse was in second place with twenty women. He said Gierse told him, "And you should see number twenty!"

To check out the rumors about pornography trafficking, the police brought back in several of the three victims' girlfriends and questioned them about it. Wava Winslow, who had dated Jim Barker, was brought in on December 21, 1971, and asked about this. She told them that she had met Barker through Diane Horton, who had been dating Bob Gierse, and that while she and Barker had had a very full sex life, she hadn't witnessed any of the men having an unusual interest in pornography. She also corroborated what Paula Palmer, Barker's ex-wife, had told Sergeant Stark: that Barker had become very unhappy at Bell and Howell because they were cutting his salary, and that he was planning to leave there and go in with Gierse and Hinson at B&B Microfilming.

However, as was becoming par for the course with this investigation, when the police requestioned Winslow they also developed yet another possible suspect. She told them about a run-in Barker and Gierse had had with a man named Frank Salonko, a former boyfriend of hers. Winslow told them that Barker and Gierse had had a confrontation with Salonko at the Idle Hour Tavern. Salonko apparently didn't like Winslow hanging around with Barker; Salonko was very possessive, and Winslow said he'd often threatened to kill her if she went out with another man. She also said he had bragged to her about shooting a man in Oklahoma. The detectives checked and found that Salonko did indeed have a police record and apparently hung out with a very rough crowd. The detectives reluctantly added him to their lengthy list of suspects.

On December 21, 1971, the police also reinterviewed Bob Gierse's girlfriend Ilene Combest. She told them that she had met Gierse about five years earlier through a girlfriend, and that she had dated him on and off ever since. Combest told the detectives that she and Gierse had had a decent sex life, though nothing to brag about, but that it had stopped completely eight months before the murders. She said that suddenly he was no longer interested in having sex with her, and he told her that it was because he was working out and lifting weights. Combest obviously didn't know about Gierse's involvement in the sex contest.

Combest additionally told the detectives that the three men didn't seem to have any special interest in pornography. Along with this, she said she had never seen any of the three men involved with or taking narcotics. (The detectives were still attempting to find out where the extra money the victims were spending was coming from, and another rumor the detectives had picked up involved the three men dealing in narcotics.) Combest did tell the police, though, that Gierse used to regularly buy stolen items from people. She said that he had bought a typewriter from a guy who often came into Records Security Corporation peddling hot items. During their investigation, the detectives had also heard from several people that the color console television set in the house on North LaSalle was stolen property, and Combest confirmed that Gierse had bought it from a guy in a Zionsville tavern.

She added that when the three victims went out somewhere they liked to throw their weight around and really enjoyed embarrassing and ridiculing people.

The conversation with Combest then turned to Gierse and Hinson's September trip to Bloomington to meet Ted Uland, a trip she had accompanied them on. She told the detectives that she had been instructed to wait in the car while Gierse and Hinson went into the Big Wheel Restaurant to talk with Uland, and that after about five minutes Hinson came back out and waited in the car with her. Uland had tried to convince Hinson to stay on at Records Security Corporation and, when he wouldn't, Uland excused him from the meeting because he said he wanted to talk to Gierse in private. When Gierse finally came out about two hours later, he told her and Hinson that Uland had offered him $10,000 to stay on at Records Security through the first of the year. But, Gierse told them, the offer was ridiculous because

Uland didn't have that kind of money. And besides, Gierse told them, no matter what, he was going to leave soon and have his own company.

However, Combest also said that both Gierse and Hinson agreed that Uland could be a dangerous man if he got backed into a corner financially. And, she said, Gierse was worried about Uland having a key to his house on North LaSalle Street because he was afraid that Uland might go down into the basement and see the equipment he planned to use in his new business. He apparently feared that Uland would recognize it.

When asked who she thought might have committed the murders, Combest said it could have been someone the men had ridiculed or pushed around in a bar, which they liked to do regularly. But, she also said, she wouldn't put it past Uland to have hired someone to do it.

Following their interview with Combest, the detectives finally located two more women on the men's scorecard of sexual conquests. One was a lady named Virginia France, who, like many others, told detectives that she had met the three victims through a girlfriend. She also denied any knowledge of the men having been involved with pornography or drugs, but did add that she had an ex-husband from whom she'd only been divorced a little over a month, and that he had serious mental problems and a violent temper. The detectives added another name to their suspect list.

On December 23, 1971, the police interviewed the second woman, Ruth Ellen Lochard. Her ex-husband, whom she had divorced in 1970, had once worked with Jim Barker, which was how she'd met him. She told the detectives that she had suspected some type of contest was going on because she said that Barker had told her she was "number thirteen." She told the detectives that she hadn't seen the men have or use any drugs, and that they hadn't shown any unusual interest in pornography.

By this point, the detectives realized that the pornography and drug-running angles were dead ends. They had just been rumors.

Although their investigation seemed not to be going anywhere, the detectives were still not ready to give up. They interviewed a Mr. Bernard M. Faust, the bookkeeper for B&B Microfilming. He gave the police an interesting bit of information. He said that Gierse instructed him not to keep a record of how much money he was paying out at B&B, an unusual request to give a bookkeeper. In a memo about the interview, though, one of the detectives noted that Faust appeared extremely nervous, had conferred with an attorney before coming to talk with the police, and could not be ruled out as a suspect himself. But interestingly enough, Faust also gave the police a new suspect, a man with a beautiful blond wife who had at one time been involved with the three victims.

On December 28, 1971, Lieutenant Joe McAtee had a meeting with Earl Timmons, an investigator for the New York Life Insurance Company, the company that had written the $150,000 key man life insurance policies on Gierse and Hinson. Timmons told McAtee that he was delaying his final report about whether New York Life should pay or not until after Uland had undergone his lie detector test, which had originally been scheduled for December 22, 1971.

However, on that date, before the scheduled test, Uland and his attorney held a four-and-a-half-hour meeting with the prosecutor in order to discuss stipulations regarding the lie detector test. The attorney had tried to cover every possible aspect of the test that might negatively affect his client, including what questions could and could not be asked. When they finally arrived at the test site, Uland's attorney refused to allow his client to sign a Miranda rights warning because he said it would conflict with the stipulations they and the prosecutor had agreed upon. Uland and his attorney then began a lengthy discussion with the detectives about the test, covering much of the same area they had already gone over with the prosecutor. By the time everything had been concluded and agreed upon, however, the test operator felt that due to possible fatigue it would be better to reschedule the lie detector test, which they did, for January 7, 1972.

Since Ted Uland had not yet taken a lie detector test, the detectives still considered him a viable suspect. However, when one of the detectives traveled to Princeton, Indiana, and spoke with Uland's secretary at Cherokee Drilling, she provided Uland with an alibi for the night of the murders. She confirmed that Uland had called Gierse long-distance from Princeton at around 9:00 P.M. Several other people additionally confirmed Uland's presence in southern Indiana on the night of November 30. Although the detectives couldn't rule out the possibility of Uland having hired someone to commit the murders for him, they had no proof or evidence of this.

Although frustrated by the lack of evidence and the continuously growing number of suspects, the detectives could not seem to stop discovering new names to add to the list. Upon interviewing one of Bob Hinson's former girlfriends, she told the detectives that the three victims had bought a lot of liquor from a bootlegger that a friend had introduced them to. However, a few months before the murders the bootlegger had stopped selling liquor to the three victims. She said the bootlegger had been arrested and that he was angry because he thought the three men might have been the ones who turned him in to the police.

On December 28, 1971, Detective Sergeant Pat Stark and a new detective to the case, Jerry Campbell, traveled to St. Louis, Missouri, to see if they could obtain any more background information on the three victims. Bob Gierse was from St. Louis, and the detectives had heard that he and the other two men would occasionally visit there. In addition, the detectives also wanted to check out rumors that the three men had been arrested the month before, in November 1971, while in St. Louis.

Upon investigation, the detectives discovered that indeed Jim Barker and Bob Hinson had been arrested in

St. Louis on November 21, 1971, for "Aiding and Abetting a Prostitute." Apparently, a nice young lady whom Barker and Hinson had shown interest in had turned out not to be such a nice young lady after all. Also, the detectives found, Barker and Hinson had been robbed by a Mordial Bailey Jr. during the same incident. Detectives Stark and Campbell were able, however, to rule Bailey out as a suspect in the murders because, ironically enough, they confirmed that on December 1, 1971, he was already in custody in St. Louis for an unrelated homicide. They also verified that he had been in St. Louis the night before. While at the St. Louis Police Department, the detectives checked seven persons of interest in the North LaSalle Street case for criminal records there, looking for any unknown connections that could help develop a motive for the murders. None of these individuals, however, had any police record in the St. Louis area.

The detectives next visited some of the nightspots the three victims would frequent while in St. Louis, figuring that if these men had liked to bully and intimidate people in Indianapolis, they'd probably liked to do it in St. Louis, too. Stark and Campbell went to the Boot Heel Club and the Pipeline Tavern, where employees recognized Jim Barker's photograph but couldn't give the detectives any useful information. Nor did the detectives have much luck at the Huckle Bee Club, the Magnolia Inn, the Olive Living Room, the Aeor Space Lounge, the Spacecraft, or the Hee Haw Club.

Detectives Stark and Campbell, a bit discouraged,

then went to speak with Gierse's sister, Dorothy Erbs, who worked at St. Joseph Hospital in Kirkwood, Missouri. She said that the last time she'd seen her brother was three months earlier, in September 1971, when he came to St. Louis to show her the new Cadillac he had bought. Erbs said that he'd brought Ilene Combest with him on the trip and told the detectives that she and her husband had jokingly referred to Combest as Gierse's "illegal wife," since she always seemed to accompany Gierse whenever he came to St. Louis. Erbs, however, wasn't able to add any new information to the investigation. She didn't know of anyone who would want to murder the men.

Following this, the detectives attempted to find Bob Gierse's ex-wife but could only locate her sister. The former sister-in-law said that the last time she had seen the victims was about six months ago in St. Louis, and that her husband had told her that Hinson was in some kind of trouble, but she didn't know what kind. The detectives knew this coincided with reports that Bob Hinson had seemed depressed and worried in the weeks before his murder. Was this connected, even though six months ago? It seemed a clue worth following up on. However, for some reason the detectives apparently didn't follow up with the sister-in-law's husband to see if he knew what kind of trouble Hinson had been in.

While in St. Louis the detectives also spoke with Bob Gierse's brother Ted, who told the detectives that the day after the murders a go-go dancer named Janice Smith, who had dated his brother, had called a friend of his and told him that the murders had been business connected and that she was afraid for her life. This was a bit of information the detectives felt needed further investigation.

Other than the news about the go-go dancer, though, the detectives returned from St. Louis with very little new information. Almost a month had passed now since the murders, and while the detectives assigned to the investigation had once thought that the case would be solved and closed by the end of the year, that didn't look like much of a possibility any longer.

An interesting development, however, did occur just before the year's end. Lieutenant McAtee reported on December 29, 1971, that a wallet belonging to Robert Hinson, which contained credit cards and identification, had been found in a yard on the west side of Indianapolis. Unfortunately, though, while this initially seemed like it could be a break in the case, the detectives soon discovered that the wallet had been stolen from Hinson some months before the murders while he lay passed out in the backseat of a car at an all-night restaurant.

The year 1971 was just about over, and most of the detectives hadn't had a day off in the month since the murders. They had worked through the Christmas holiday, and it looked as though they were going to work through New Year's also. It was unbelievably frustrating. The detectives knew only too well that the reason they couldn't solve this case was because they simply didn't have the physical evidence or witness testimony that could break one suspect away from the rest. They hadn't been able to connect the bloody footprint or the cigar to any suspect. But a break had to come soon, they knew—a surprise eyewitness, someone who heard something, or an unknown piece of physical evidence—for if it didn't, it appeared this case might never be solved.

CHAPTER FIVE

New Year's Day 1972 had come and gone. Most of the homicide detectives assigned to the North LaSalle Street case had worked through the holiday, but the leads they followed kept running dry. The original detectives had now worked forty-five days straight without a day off. They had taken recorded statements from 150 people and had interviewed 600 others, including 36 in St. Louis, 30 in Chicago, and 180 of the victims' business associates and customers.

In a January 1972 article in the *Indianapolis Star*, Deputy Chief Ralph Lumpkin said that while the police were still looking at the murders as being a crime of passion, they were also now looking at a business/social motive. In actuality, however, the detectives were stumped.

Also in early January 1972, the detectives had a crime lab technician remove the sink trap from the bathroom on North LaSalle Street and analyze its contents. The detectives knew they needed physical evidence desperately. There was the possibility that the murderer or murderers might have used the sink to clean up afterward since they had likely gotten blood on them, but also, the detectives hoped, they might have washed out a wound of their own. Nothing of significance, though, came of this.

"I wish we'd had DNA in those days," Popcheff would say years after the murder investigation. "It sure would have made it a lot easier." Had the murders occurred today, the detective assigned to the case would have had a DNA sample taken from the cigar butt found in the dining room and then run this sample through the Combined DNA Index System (CODIS), the FBI's national link of state DNA banks. If the person who had committed the murders had been arrested for a felony anywhere in the United States, and consequently a DNA sample taken, a match would come up and an arrest would be made. But unfortunately, 1971 was decades before such technology existed, let alone was linked by databases nationwide.

By mid-January 1972, the news media had finally lost interest in the case. While for several weeks following the crime there had been front-page articles or breaking newscasts every day about the murders, the coverage had finally dried up. After the initial rush of news stories, a case with no progress and no arrests didn't stir much interest. The news media eventually turned to other topics of importance in the early 1970s.

SLAUGHTER ON NORTH LASALLE 115

But worst of all, as far as the investigators were concerned, even though the case had initially looked like it wouldn't be that hard to solve, and even though police officials had announced several times that a solution and arrests were imminent, the detectives knew that they weren't any closer to solving the case than they had been on the day it occurred. The three men, with their stolen equipment and customers, their shady business dealings, their rowdy sex lives, and their enjoyment of embarrassing and pushing people around, had dozens of people who might have wanted to see them dead. But what had really stumped the detectives and stalled the investigation was the lack of substantial hard evidence, which left many questions unanswered.

"It seemed like we just couldn't get our hands on anything in this case," said Popcheff. "For example, something was missing from Gierse's nightstand, but we never could find out what it was. Another question we had was: who went out the back door and left it open? We couldn't find out. We just couldn't get the upper hand on this case."

But regardless, the detectives knew that they couldn't quit as long as there was any trail at all left to follow. And so, in early January 1972, they went to the Warren hotel in downtown Indianapolis to look for the go-go dancer that Bob's brother Ted Gierse had mentioned. Unfortunately, but not unexpectedly, when the detectives arrived, they found that several of the go-go dancers who worked in the bar at the hotel had been acquainted with the three victims. Each one had a theory about what had happened.

None of them, though, were able to give investigators any really new or relevant information about the case.

Eventually, though, the detectives located Geneva Darlene Smith, nicknamed Janice, the go-go dancer who had called Ted Gierse's friend in St. Louis the day after the murders. She told the detectives that she had dated Bob Gierse for four or five months and then started dating Bob Hinson. Smith said she had never dated Jim Barker, though he *had* tried to get her to go out with him several times. When asked why she had called Ted Gierse's friend right after the murders, Smith told the detectives that she had called because she and Hinson had double-dated with the friend when he was in Indianapolis and realized that he had known the three victims very well. As to the reason for the killings, she remembered saying that the triple murder had been business related, but couldn't give the police any concrete evidence for her belief.

As might be imagined, since the day of the murders, tips on the case had come in from all corners. Even if the news media had lost interest in the case, much of the public hadn't. The murders were still the topic of conversation in many bars and around many watercoolers. Consequently, individuals who thought they had heard something incriminating or had suddenly come up with a clue would call the police. Naturally, any of these tips that had any credibility at all had to be checked out, and that task took up hour after hour of the detectives' time.

Most of these tips, though, turned out to be a waste of time.

A woman who worked at the White Metal Company in Indianapolis, for example, called in to say that she thought another woman who worked there might have been at the North LaSalle Street house on the night of the murders. As it turned out, when the detectives investigated this tip they found that the woman had based her information solely on the fact that the other woman talked constantly about the murders with other workers.

One of the suspects in the case, Ted Uland, came to a meeting with the prosecutor's staff before his scheduled lie detector test in January and, after being advised of his Miranda rights, agreed to talk about what he knew of the triple murder. None of the homicide detectives assigned to the North LaSalle Street case were at this meeting, but they did receive a transcript of it later. Uland told the prosecutor's staff that he had come in because he'd had several reporters calling him, but that he just didn't feel comfortable talking to them. Also, he said he had come in because he was worried that maybe one of his employees at Records Security Corporation might be blamed for the murders. He didn't want someone to take a potshot at them.

The first thing Uland wanted was to be certain the people at the meeting knew that he had called long-distance from southern Indiana and talked with Gierse and Hinson on the night of the murders. He didn't know if the call went to the office of B&B Microfilming on East 10th Street or to the house on North LaSalle Street.

(Gierse had his phone system set up so that it would ring in both places.) Uland said that he had also called earlier in the afternoon about a quote Gierse had been involved with concerning microfilming and records storage for a hospital in Danville, Indiana. His new manager at Records Security Corporation apparently couldn't find the quote, and Uland thought that Gierse might know where it was. He said that he'd also wanted to ask Gierse about a $600 check he had written on the Records Security Corporation account. Uland said Gierse told him to call back later that evening after he'd had time to look at his records.

Uland told the group that he called back at around 9:00 P.M. and first spoke with Hinson, who said that Gierse was out getting sandwiches and that he should call back in about a half hour. At 9:30 P.M., Uland said, he called back and talked to Gierse. They straightened out the matter of the missing quote and then, he said, Gierse told him that he had used the $600 check to pay some of his personal bills. Uland told the prosecutor's staff that Gierse claimed he had put some of his personal money into the company to make up the payroll and that this was just him being repaid. Uland told the prosecutor's staff that he then said okay and hung up, and that was the last time he ever spoke to either man.

An investigator who reviewed the transcript of this meeting wrote in the margin: "Pretty nonchalant about $600!" The investigator also noted: "Uland called Gierse to make sure he was home?"

When asked how he felt about Gierse and Hinson leaving Records Security Corporation to start their own company, Uland told the prosecutor's staff that it had caught him completely by surprise. He said he first learned about it when he found out that an important client of his had signed with a new company. This was the same day, he said, that Hinson resigned, a few weeks before Gierse would. Uland claimed Hinson told him that a company named Technifax had gotten the contract and that he was going to work for them, when in actuality he was leaving to start up B&B Microfilming, who had really gotten the contract.

Uland went on to tell the prosecutor's staff that Gierse also said he was considering leaving the company. Uland then talked about the meeting at the Big Wheel Restaurant in Bloomington, and how at the meeting he had tried to convince Hinson to stay on at Records Security, but wasn't successful. Hinson told him that he had definitely decided to go with Technifax. He said that Gierse then told him that he hadn't decided yet whether he was leaving Records Security, but that Technifax had made him an offer he was considering. (In a strange coincidence, Lafayette Robert Roe, the man whose stolen car had turned up with blood in it the day after the murders, worked for Technifax, which owned Scott Graphics.) Uland told the prosecutor's staff that he believed both men respected him so much that neither one could tell him the truth: that they were leaving to start their own business.

Following this, Uland then went on to talk about how he had just found out that some of the equipment the police had recovered at B&B Microfilming actually belonged to him and that it was the same equipment Gierse had claimed was taken in a burglary. He also told them that he thought Gierse and Hinson might have ripped him off for over $10,000 by writing checks that looked as though they were for business purposes, but which the two men had actually cashed themselves. The prosecutor's staff was puzzled because Uland seemed very nonchalant about the missing money. The investigator reviewing the transcript wrote in the margin next to the comment about the $10,000: "Why wasn't Uland mad?"

They then talked about the key man life insurance policies on Gierse and Hinson. Uland told the prosecutor's staff that he hoped the policies weren't in effect, because if they were it would put him in a bad light. The investigator wrote in the margin: "No kidding!"

Uland next related how, since Gierse and Hinson knew all of the customers who used Records Security Corporation, they had been able to persuade these companies to change their business to B&B Microfilming. Uland also told the prosecutor's staff about work that was supposed to be coming in to Records Security Corporation that had been secretly diverted to B&B. Most of the people at the meeting thought it strange that Uland told this very matter-of-factly and didn't seem surprised or upset that the two men would do this, even though it cost his company dearly.

During the questioning, Uland also brought up the possibility that Gierse and Hinson might have been working on classified material. However, he said he didn't have any personal knowledge of this, only what one of his employees had told him. Uland also talked about having $5,500 in an account that was supposed to be sent to the Internal Revenue Service for quarterly taxes, and how Gierse had sent in the forms but not the money. When he checked the account recently, Uland said that he found it had no money in it. The investigator made a note in the margin: "Uland thought Gierse cleaned out accounts!"

Finally, Uland added another suspect to the already long list of jealous exes: He told the prosecutor's staff about a woman whom Bob Hinson had dated, who lived only a street or two over from North LaSalle. Uland claimed Hinson had laughed about it and told him that she had a very jealous ex-husband who had threatened to kill him.

The interview finally ended, leaving many on the prosecutor's staff feeling suspicious. Uland had admitted during the questioning that, because of what his former employees Gierse and Hinson had done, his company was now on very shaky financial grounds. He had been taken advantage of in a big way by Gierse and Hinson, yet didn't seem visibly upset about it. He appeared cool— much *too* cool. Uland closed by telling the prosecutor's staff how very close he had been to both Gierse and Hinson and how they had been like family to him. The investigator wrote in the margin: "If so close, why would they leave his company, steal money, equipment, and accounts?" The investigator also wrote: "What happened to [Uland's] key to [the house on North] LaSalle Street?"

However, the people at the meeting also knew that Uland had a solid alibi for the night of the murders; one that the phone company and witnesses would back up.

The prosecutor's staff closed the meeting realizing that the detectives had no firm evidence against Uland, or for that matter against any of the other multitude of suspects who had come up in the thousands of hours the police department had put into the case. Consequently, soon after this, the investigation began to slow down. It had been more than a month, with much searching but no progress, and new murders had since occurred that needed investigation. The detectives and prosecutor's staff turned their attention to concentrating on these.

No one in law enforcement forgot about the North LaSalle Street case, especially not the original investigating detectives, but there wasn't anything left they could do. They had followed hundreds of leads, talked to hundreds of witnesses, and interrogated dozens of suspects. But nothing had clicked. The detectives could see nothing that pointed to any one person as the most likely candidate. All of the original detectives hoped that someday new evidence or an unknown witness would show up. But until then, the case would lay cold.

A little over a year after the murders, New York Life Insurance Company finally paid off the $150,000 worth of key man life insurance policies Ted Uland had held on Bob Gierse and Bob Hinson. The insurance company had had no choice, since the policies had still been in effect and Uland had never been officially charged. Indianapolis Police Department records show that Lieutenant McAtee, on December 5, 1972, approved release of the insurance policies to Uland's attorney.

Although the Homicide Branch eventually pulled the detectives away from the North LaSalle Street case and assigned them new cases to work on, of course the detectives still wanted to eventually see it solved. And so, in July 1973, still desperate to figure out what had happened during the murders, the Indianapolis Police Department brought in Ross Peterson, a well-known psychic, to look at the case. When the news media heard about this, they naturally wanted to know all of the details. Deputy Chief Lumpkin reluctantly admitted to the press that they had brought in Peterson to see if he could offer any help in a case that, according to the *Indianapolis Star*, "has baffled the police because of its incredible butchery and the lack of concrete leads."

However, while Deputy Chief Lumpkin may have thought calling in Peterson was worth a try, not everyone in the Indianapolis Police Department agreed with him. The new head of the Homicide Branch, Captain Robert Greene, made no secret of his dislike for the idea and what a waste of time he felt it to be. Greene believed in chasing concrete leads. For example, he would have his detectives periodically check with other police departments whenever similar murders occurred.

Still, psychics offering help in criminal investigations is fairly common in law enforcement. Every time a major crime occurs, generating a lot of publicity, police depart-

ments will have many self-proclaimed psychics, sometimes dozens of them, calling in with their visions of
what happened. Most police departments are very skeptical of psychics, usually because all they provide is very
general information, such as "I see the victim's body. It's
buried in a cornfield." (In Indiana, at least, this isn't really that helpful.) A lot of these "psychics" are looking
for publicity; they know that all they need is one lucky
guess that solves a high-profile crime and they are set for
life. Psychic Jeane Dixon was able to propel her predic-
tion (or lucky guess) of John F. Kennedy's death into a
lifetime of celebrity status. Detectives, however, don't
want guesses; they want facts, they want addresses, they
want directions to where the body is. With the large ma-
jority of "psychics," however, they don't get this.

Peterson, according to news reports, climbed up and
then stretched out on a conference table at police headquarters and went into what he called a theta trance. Peterson claimed not to know what he was saying when he was
in a trance, and said he only found out later when he listened to a tape recording of it. His take on the North
LaSalle Street murders was certainly different from the
other directions the case had taken; he said that because
the men were having such serious financial troubles with
their new business, they had decided to raise money by
selling drugs that a woman was supposed to bring them
from Mexico. But when, according to Peterson, mobsters
in Chicago heard about the drug deal, they set up a hit
through contacts in New York City and Detroit because
the men were apparently trespassing on the Mob's turf.

"This guy climbs up on the table and lays there, then starts talking in a monotone voice," said Popcheff. "He claimed to be able to see the car parked outside the crime scene, so I asked him to give us the license plate number. He couldn't."

However, not all psychics are dismissed by police departments. Sometimes—though very, very seldom—psychics have been able to give the police some insight into what happened. Whether this is the result of simply an educated guess or an actual psychic vision, police don't care, as long as the information is usable.

Naturally, a crime as brutal as the North LaSalle Street case generated a number of articles in detective magazines. Most of these articles focused on the sex aspect of the case or on the brutality of the murders. Some, however, looked for a solution. For example, according to the magazine *True Police Cases*, psychic David Hoy offered his unsolicited help in the case, saying he didn't think the case involved any jealous husbands or boyfriends, but rather that the murders had been business related. According to Hoy, a businessman had warned Gierse and Hinson to stop making waves, but they'd ignored him. The businessman then hired two men to kill Gierse and Hinson. Barker was killed simply because he was in the wrong place at the wrong time. Finally, Hoy said, the man who had contracted the killings soon began suffering from depression, and he believed the individual would eventually confess.

* * *

Because the murders had been such a highly publicized case, the Indianapolis Police Department had a number of people, even years after the murders, who wanted to confess to them. With just a little questioning, though, the police were soon able to confirm that the person only knew what he or she had learned through the news media.

For example, the police received an anonymous call from a man who told the policewoman who answered the telephone that he was the one who had killed the three men on North LaSalle Street. He told her that he'd only wanted to kill Bob Hinson because Hinson had been sleeping with his wife. He said word of this indiscretion had gotten around to some of the taverns he went to on the east side of Indianapolis, and so he'd had no choice but to kill him. The man then hung up and the police were unable to trace the call. This type of thing went on for years.

False confessions, however, weren't the only information the police department would receive about the case in the years afterward. While the local news media may have moved on to other news, and the police detectives on to new murder cases, the North LaSalle Street murders continued to hold the attention of many people in Indianapolis, even years later. For example, Indianapolis police Sergeant Darryl Churchill sent an interdepartment communication on February 3, 1975, to the Homicide Branch saying that he had an informant who told him that the men on North LaSalle Street had been killed over a woman. In addition, he said, his informant told him that a woman the police had recently found murdered near Greenfield, Indiana, had been killed because she knew the truth about the North LaSalle Street murders and was going to talk.

In 1978, Marion County Prosecutor James Kelley passed on information from a confidential informant about three men possibly involved in the North LaSalle Street case. However, two of the men had already been suspects but had been cleared. The third man was an enforcer for the Teamsters Union, but the police could find no connection between him and the North LaSalle Street murders. Detective Sergeant Popcheff asked Prosecutor Kelley if he could have the name of the informant so that he could talk with him, but Kelley wouldn't release the name. In the years following the murders, the police department received many tips such as this from criminal informants, but nothing came of them.

In 1980, the North LaSalle Street case was temporarily reopened when the police located a woman who had stayed at the North LaSalle Street house on November 29, 1971, the day before the murders. The police found out about her through her boyfriend, who, upon discovering this nearly decade-old piece of information, became bitterly jealous and called the police. Detectives brought the woman in for questioning, but she had nothing useful to tell them. She said that everything had seemed peaceful and normal at the house while she was there. The police department deactivated the case again.

And while the news media's interest in the North LaSalle Street murders had naturally waned, they also never

totally forgot the case. For a number of years, on the
anniversary of the murders, the media would revive the
events and bring them back to the public's mind. For
example, on December 1, 1983, the twelfth anniversary
of the murders, a columnist for the *Indianapolis Star*
wrote an article about them, noting that although Ted
Uland was the only person of interest to never take a lie
detector test, lead detective Joe McAtee (who by 1983
was the chief of police) said he felt that the murders were
connected to the men's sexual contest, and that the reason the police department hadn't solved the case was
because they were never able to get a complete list of
these women. (Apparently, the men had been murdered
before they could finish entering in November's sexual
conquests.)

Another resurrection of the case occurred in 1984. A
woman called the police in July of that year and said that
a man she knew by the name of David LaFever had come
by her house the night after the murders in 1971 and
told her that he had just completed a job for some people
and that it was one of the worst things he could have
done. He told her he had been instructed to get back
something these people had, and that he had been paid
very well, but now he had to disappear for a while. He
said he wouldn't have to worry about money for a long
time.

The woman said that LaFever called her two weeks
later, and from time to time afterward, always asking her
what the police had found out about the murders on

North LaSalle Street. She said he would kind of chuckle about it. The woman told the police that LaFever would have her save and read him articles out of the paper about the murders. She also said that LaFever and Bob Hinson had been friends, and that LaFever had brought Hinson over to her house a few days before the murders. The woman said she didn't know Hinson, but that LaFever had later told her that's who it had been.

This woman also told the police that though LaFever never came out and admitted he had actually committed the murders, he liked to hint that he had. He would, for example, explain to her how one person could manage to kill all three of these men by himself. She also said that LaFever had always been fascinated by martial arts and stealth killing. The police, though certainly looking into this report, didn't attach much importance to it. Since the murders, they had received reports of many men who had bragged to women they wanted to either scare or impress that they had committed the North LaSalle Street murders.

In early July 1985, however, the Coconino County Superior Court in Flagstaff, Arizona, sentenced David LaFever to twelve years in prison for sexually molesting his twelve-year-old adopted daughter. His wife Margaret received a two-year sentence for "Facilitating the Sexual Exploitation of a Minor." Soon after the sentencing, David contacted the authorities and told them that he wanted to discuss the triple murder on North LaSalle Street in exchange for a more lenient sentence for Margaret. The police in Indianapolis were getting ready to fly out to Arizona to talk with David when he suddenly changed his mind about wanting to discuss the case. At the end of the day, the police believed he'd probably been hoping to fabricate a story that would help his wife but then realized he would either have to come up with facts he didn't have or implicate himself in it. But just in case, the police compared David's fingerprints with the unidentified fingerprints from the North LaSalle Street case. No match was found.

Most distressingly, on June 8, 1984, a sergeant from the Homicide Branch—for some unknown reason—signed off to have much of the evidence in the case destroyed, including microfilm, address books, the bloody bedsheets, large quantities of written material, several knives, pieces of cord, checks, and bank statements. He did this despite the fact that evidence in murder cases is supposed to be held until the case is finally solved, the defendant convicted, and the appeals exhausted. How this oversight could have happened was baffling, especially since the words MURDER CASE were stamped in large, bold letters on the property room form specifically to prevent such a thing from occurring.

Naturally, the original detectives in the case, though they had long since moved on to new cases, had never given up hope of being able to perhaps one day solve the North LaSalle Street case. Detective Sergeant Strode, when he heard the news about the evidence destruction, fired off a memo to the chief of police asking how this could have happened on an open murder case and pointing out how this action could cripple any future attempts to solve the case.

Although this incident upset many people, no one in the police department considered it an act of corruption or collusion with the killers. Police department property rooms routinely become so full of evidence and confiscated property that the officer in charge of the property room will send out disposition notices to the officers, telling them to come down and either dispose of the evidence or signal that it is still needed. Apparently, the North LaSalle Street evidence simply got mixed up with the wrong cases.

Fortunately, a small amount of the evidence, two of four original boxes of clothing and some of the blood and autopsy samples, had not yet been destroyed, and the detectives managed to recover them. They also recovered some of the microfilm and several pieces of microfilm equipment.

In 1987, sixteen years after the murders, an employee of the state parole board received information that a former go-go dancer by the name of Margo (or possibly Margaret) had information about the triple murder on North LaSalle Street. This woman, the man said, now worked at the Golden Palace Bar.

It was enough of a lead for the police department to detail Popcheff, now working as a lieutenant in uniformed patrol, back to the Homicide Branch. Popcheff, still hopeful of solving the North LaSalle Street murders, located Margo, who told him that at the time of the murders she and her boyfriend had been managing Tommy's Starlight Palladium Bar, then owned by a local crime figure named Norman Flick. Margo told Popcheff that she believed Flick had possibly been involved in the North LaSalle Street murders. Local burglar Bobby Atkinson, a cousin of hers, she said, was a suspect in the John Terhorst murder and was then murdered himself. She thought that Atkinson had sold Gierse and Hinson some stolen microfilm machines. She had no proof of this but still believed it. Margo said that right after the triple murder two men from out of town came into Tommy's Starlight Palladium Bar and talked with Flick for some time, but then soon left town. She believed they may have been involved in the North LaSalle Street murders. Again, she had no proof, only her belief that it was so. One of the men, Margo said, had "dark, hateful eyes." Popcheff had the Identification Branch compare the fingerprints of the men Margo mentioned as possibly being involved in the North LaSalle Street killings against the unidentified fingerprints from North LaSalle Street. The technician found no match.

Margo said that when she heard of the murders she called the Homicide Branch, but they thought she was crazy and wouldn't talk to her. Margo said she also called the local newspaper, which sent out two reporters. However, since no news stories about her had appeared in 1971, Popcheff suspected that they hadn't believed her. Indeed, when contacted later, one of the reporters said that he hadn't considered her a very reliable source, because she was so weird, making wild claims with no proof.

Following this, Popcheff lost contact with Margo. He

said in his report that she had agreed to meet with him again, but then never did. Popcheff wrote of his meeting with Margo that while she might have been of some help in 1971, he felt that she had forgotten too many details in the years since then. Popcheff sent his report in to the deputy chief of investigations and then went back to his assignment as a uniformed street lieutenant.

This case, however, simply wouldn't let go of him. In an article in the *Indianapolis News* in 1992, more than two decades after the murders, Popcheff would say that the crime had stumped police because it had had no eyewitnesses and far too many possible motives. He said they'd tried to find nearly one hundred women who had been involved with one or all of the three men. Despite the optimism of the detectives in 1971, the North La-Salle Street case sat unsolved in the cold case file for twenty years.

In 1991, however, a beautiful young reporter took an interest in the murders. She began her own investigation and soon brought the case back into the media spotlight.

PART TWO
1991

CHAPTER SIX

In 1991, a very attractive journalist in her late twenties named Carol Schultz wrote a feature article for the *Indianapolis News* about bounty hunters. The article went on to garner Schultz a journalism award and high praise from her editor. Naturally, she wanted a repeat of this.

Schultz knew, however, that she had to come up with a really good subject if she was going to follow up on her earlier success. After quite a bit of thought and investigation, Schultz found out that the television program *Unsolved Mysteries* was filming in Fort Wayne, Indiana, a town about 125 miles northeast of Indianapolis. And so, she decided to write a piece for the newspaper about the person they were profiling on the program.

As she became involved in writing that article, Schultz also began to wonder about whether there were any unsolved mysteries closer to home, in Indianapolis. What, she asked herself, was Indianapolis's greatest unsolved mystery? Eventually, a librarian at the Indianapolis Marion County Public Library pointed Schultz toward the North LaSalle Street murders, still unsolved, and whose twentieth anniversary would be coming up in December of that year. The librarian told Schultz it was a fascinating case and that she should read up on it.

Schultz began researching the murders and soon found herself indeed fascinated by the case. It had everything she needed for a feature article: sex, death, and mystery, wrapped in the story of three handsome, virile men who were brutally murdered. The case, she found, had enthralled the public for some time in the early 1970s, and everyone she talked to confirmed that the North LaSalle Street murders were definitely the biggest unsolved mystery in the history of Indianapolis. With just a little reading on the case, Schultz found that the police had committed thousands of man-hours to the investigation, but no solution had materialized. Schultz also discovered that theories about the perpetrators had numbered in the dozens, making the case even more complicated and mysterious. With its twenty-year anniversary in the near future, Schultz knew she could get some good play from her editor on the idea of a feature article about the murders; once she got approval, she knew she needed to begin some really in-depth research on the case.

In a book she later wrote, Schultz said that one of the first things she did when she started her research was to call and arrange a meeting with Lieutenant Michael Popcheff, one of the original detectives who had investigated the North LaSalle Street murders in 1971. Popcheff had then been a detective sergeant in homicide, but in 1991 he was a lieutenant working in uniform on the south side of Indianapolis. Popcheff agreed to meet with her at a Waffle House restaurant on East Washington Street, about six or seven miles from the original murder scene.

Popcheff later said he regretted agreeing to that meeting. "Carol Schultz called me at roll call and said she would like to do a story about the LaSalle Street case," he said. "I said okay, no big deal. That was a mistake." Popcheff regretted meeting with her because Schultz eventually began subscribing to an extremely elaborate conspiracy theory in the North LaSalle Street killings that didn't fit any of the information or evidence the detectives had uncovered in 1971.

Popcheff said that during their meeting at the Waffle House, they discussed what the detectives had seen and done at the murder scene, and then they talked about how hard all of the detectives had worked on the case. Popcheff told her about the detectives missing Christmas and New Year's with their families to stay on the investigation, and about how he had even missed his sister's wedding because he wanted to stay on the case. He also told her about chasing down the hundreds and hundreds of leads that came into the police department, almost all of which led nowhere.

During the meeting, Schultz claims that Popcheff also told her that he had a new clue as to what might have actually happened on North LaSalle Street, but that the police department wouldn't give him permission to investigate it. He then, according to Schultz, suggested to her that she check it out, telling her that he had recently run into a witness in the murder case named Margo, who in 1971 had worked at a tavern in Indianapolis called Tommy's Starlight Palladium Bar. This was the hangout, he said, for a minor organized crime figure in the 1970s named Norman Flick. Popcheff then told her the witness said that on the night of the murders a man with "dark, evil, crazy" eyes had come into the bar and spoken with Flick. Margo believed that this man had been involved in the North LaSalle Street murders at the order of Norman Flick.

Schultz's version of this story was interesting, though it diverged from the report Popcheff wrote for the homicide case file about his interview with this Margo, and what she told him. Popcheff had ended his report by saying that he didn't think Margo could be of any assistance in solving the North LaSalle Street murders. And quite differently from Schultz's claim that Popcheff told her he was unable to get permission from the police department to check out this lead, the police department had actually pulled Popcheff off of uniformed duty and detailed him back to the Homicide Branch specifically in order to do so.

Popcheff would later say that he recalled telling Schultz about the information concerning Margo, but not telling her that she should investigate it herself.

However, Margo apparently wasn't the only person

to have seen this man with the "dark, evil, crazy" eyes. Schultz and Popcheff also talked about Michael Ray, the young man who'd been walking home from his brother's house along North LaSalle Street on the night of the murders and had told the police he'd seen a car sitting across the street from the crime scene. According to an article written by her in *NUVO*, Schultz claims that Popcheff said this witness also told the police that one of the men sitting in the car had "dark, evil, crazy" eyes. Schultz couldn't believe it was a coincidence and thought that this had to be the same man that Margo had talked about. (It's unclear where this idea came from, since the report in the homicide case file of what Ray told the police about the car and its occupants on the night of the murders didn't contain any reference to "dark, evil, crazy" eyes.) Nevertheless, Schultz knew that if she was ever going to solve the North LaSalle Street case, she'd have to find out who this man was.

Schultz took all of the information she had gotten from Popcheff and, combining it with the other research she had done, wrote a feature article about the twentieth anniversary of the greatest unsolved murder case in the state of Indiana's history. Her article ran on the front page of the *Indianapolis News* on November 30, 1991, and garnered Schultz some good attention from her editor, and apparently a good response from readers. Still, she couldn't help but keep thinking about the clue Popcheff had given her. The case fascinated her, and she knew that the articles she had written so far would be only minor sidebars compared to the coverage she would get if she could solve the twenty-year-old mystery. But to do this, Schultz realized she needed to find both Margo and Michael Ray. She felt certain they could lead her to the man with the "dark, evil, crazy" eyes.

After an extensive search, Schultz wrote in an article for *NUVO*, she eventually found Ray, then living in Michigan, and spoke with him about what he had seen that night on North LaSalle Street. (However, neither in the article nor in her book does Schultz say exactly what he told her during the conversation.) Next, Schultz set out to find the woman named Margo, whom she said she eventually located working at a run-down bar in Indianapolis. Again, neither in the article nor in her book does Schultz note precisely what Margo told her, and whether or not she confirmed the information about the man with the strange eyes.

(Interestingly, in Schultz's book where she talks of her early investigation of the North LaSalle Street murders, she also claimed to have found information stating that the FBI and the CIA had been called into the case the day after John Karnes found the bodies. However, she didn't mention where she got that information. The only reference to either of these organizations in the homicide case file was regarding sending some evidence to the FBI Laboratory several weeks after the murders; there is no reference to the Indianapolis Police Department asking either of those organizations for assistance in the actual investigation. It would have been odd if they had, since it was a murder case and no federal laws had been broken. Schultz also claimed that the CIA may have attended the funeral services for the three men, and that both they and the FBI were baffled by the case. Again, however, Schultz doesn't note where that information came from.)

Still intent on her story, Schultz then set out to find Norman Flick, the owner of Tommy's Starlight Palladium Bar and the individual whom the man with the strange eyes had presumably talked to. In his report to the Homicide Branch, Popcheff said that Margo had believed Flick and this man had been involved in the North LaSalle Street killings. Some years earlier, however, Flick had been convicted and sent to a federal prison. So Schultz wrote a letter to him and sent it to the penitentiary. Flick answered her letter and then reportedly called her on the telephone. Schultz said that he denied everything, not only having anything to do with the North LaSalle Street murders, but he even denied owning Tommy's Starlight Palladium Bar.

After having conducted these interviews, Schultz's next step was to meet again with Lieutenant Popcheff to tell him what she had uncovered. They again met at the Waffle House. In her book, Schultz claims that Popcheff seemed amazed at what she had found out and complimented her on her story in the newspaper. She said that he seemed completely in awe of what she had done and uncovered in such a short time. Then, according to Schultz, Popcheff produced the telephone and address book that had contained the victims' scorecard of

sexual conquests, which Schultz said Popcheff let her
touch and look at. Following this, she said, he also
handed her Gierse's bankbook to examine.

Popcheff then, Schultz said, told her that if she really
wanted to solve the case she had to find out the identity
of the man with the strange eyes. He suggested that she
research some of the dozens of newspaper articles that
had been written about the case to see if she could find
a clue about his identity. Schultz said she asked him if
he thought it would be helpful if she found some of the
old girlfriends of the three victims. Popcheff thought
it might, she said, because all they did when the police
talked to them in 1971 was cry. (Apparently, according
to her, he made no mention of the pages of notes in the
homicide files detailing the extensive interviews with
these women.) Schultz said that she and Popcheff then
met every Saturday at the Waffle House for the next year.

Soon after their conversation about the man with the
strange eyes, Schultz claims, Popcheff took her down to
the Homicide Branch of the Indianapolis Police Department, where he introduced her to the homicide commander and managed to get her access to the case file for
the North LaSalle Street murders. Schultz said that she
then sat down and read the file while the homicide commander brought her a collection of crime scene photos to
review, which she said both horrified and fascinated her.
Schultz claims it took several hours to read through the
case file and take notes, but she finally completed it and
gave it back to the homicide commander. Interestingly,
in her book, Schultz said that the North LaSalle Street

Robert Gierse

Robert Hinson

James Barker

Crime lab technician wheeling evidence-collecting equipment into the crime scene at 1318 North LaSalle Street, a residence shared by Bob Gierse and Bob Hinson. They and their good friend Jim Barker were all found dead there on the morning of December 1, 1971.

Diane Horton, girlfriend of victim Bob Gierse, is consoled by a friend at the murder scene.

B&B Microfilming Service Company, the business founded by Gierse and Hinson, had recently gotten off to an amazingly successful start.

Louise Cole, secretary at B&B Microfilming Service Company, couldn't believe what had happened to her bosses.

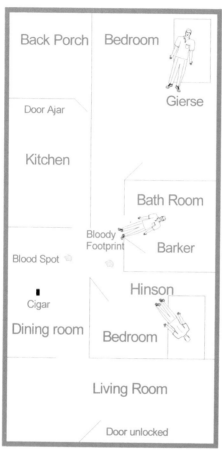

Back Porch

Bedroom

Gierse

Door Ajar

Kitchen

Bath Room

Bloody
Footprint

Barker

Blood Spot

Cigar

Hinson

Dining room

Bedroom

Living Room

Door unlocked

LaSalle
Street
Crime
Scene

Crime scene diagram of 1318 North LaSalle Street.   *ROBERT L. SNOW*

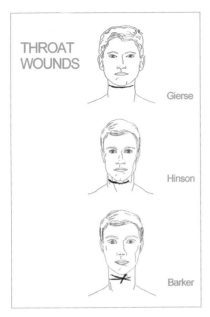

Autopsy drawings of the throat wounds. Barker's throat wound in particular shows that, even though bound, he likely struggled with his assailant.

ROBERT L. SNOW

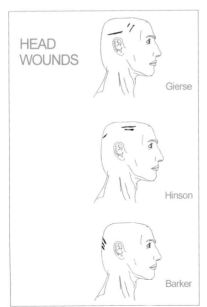

Autopsy drawings of the head wounds. The diagrams support the belief that the victims were surprised and attacked from the rear.

ROBERT L. SNOW

Carroll Horton, ex-husband to one of the victims' girlfriends, became a key suspect when the case was re-opened in the mid-1990s.

GARY MOORE/ THE INDIANAPOLIS STAR

Floyd Chastain claimed to have been at the crime scene, and implicated Carroll Horton in the murders.

GARY MOORE/ THE INDIANAPOLIS STAR

Carol Schultz, investigative reporter for a local newspaper, resurrected the North LaSalle Street case in the mid-1990s.

GARY MOORE/ THE INDIANAPOLIS STAR

Joseph McAtee headed up the police investigation of the murders in 1971 as a Detective Lieutenant, and re-opened the case in the 1990s when he was sheriff of Marion County.

Detective Sergeant Roy West solved the North LaSalle Street murders thirty years after they were discovered.

THE INDIANAPOLIS METROPOLITAN POLICE DEPARTMENT

Detective Sergeant Roy West at the New York City Morgue after the 9/11 tragedy. *COURTESY OF ROY WEST*

case file was contained in a black ledger about a foot thick. This is puzzling, because the Indianapolis Police Department keeps its homicide case files in storage boxes, not ledgers.

Schultz also says in her memories of her investigation that Popcheff watched her closely the entire time she reviewed the file, apparently to be certain that she didn't try to take anything. She was allowed to take notes, but she couldn't have any of the documents from the file. Schultz said Popcheff was always extremely careful like that, and that whenever the two of them met at the Waffle House, he would even take items with him if he had to get up to use the bathroom, again apparently to be certain she didn't try to take anything. (Popcheff, however, doesn't recall these events involving evidence from the case.)

Following her trip to the Homicide Office, Schultz said she followed Popcheff's recommendation and visited the microfilm room of the Indianapolis Marion County Public Library. There, she began researching all of the old newspaper articles about the North LaSalle Street murders, discovering that for several weeks in December 1971, an article about the murders had appeared almost every day on the front page of the city's two newspapers. She also found that a number of the articles had been written by one reporter in particular, a man named Dick Cady. When she called him, though, Schultz said in an article in *NUVO* and in her book, Cady really didn't want to talk to her because he claimed that he had already solved the murders and had written several articles about it in 1977. When she asked him why, if he had solved them, the police hadn't made any arrests yet, he told her that the press and the police didn't work together in Indianapolis, and that she needed to read all of the articles he had written before she called him again.

What Cady said about the lack of cooperation between the local newspapers and the police in Indianapolis was true. It stemmed from a series of newspaper articles lasting over a year that the *Indianapolis Star* had published in the mid 1970s about alleged corruption within the Indianapolis Police Department. Most of the department's officers felt that the articles were totally unfair and unsubstantiated, pointing to the fact that no one was ever indicted or convicted as a result of this assault on the police department's reputation. The *Indianapolis Star*, on the other hand, pointed out that they won a Pulitzer Prize because of the series. Both sides thought they were right, and the distrust lasted for years.

Cady's articles about the North LaSalle Street case claimed that it had been three men with serious criminal pasts who had committed the murders. Cady had even included photos of the three men in his articles. To her surprise, Schultz found that one of the men pictured had "dark, evil, crazy" eyes.

Schultz says she met with Popcheff again at the Waffle House and felt very disappointed that he didn't seem nearly as excited as she was about finding the man. She said he was more angry at Cady's claim that he had solved the North LaSalle Street murders. The distrust between reporters and the police still lingered. To cut the tension,

Schultz suggested that maybe she could call the producers of *Unsolved Mysteries* and see if she could get them interested in doing a segment on the North LaSalle Street murders. A program like that could bring out witnesses who might, even after all of these years, have information that could help in solving the case.

According to Schultz, when she made the call, the producer of *Unsolved Mysteries* seemed very interested in doing a segment about the murders but stipulated that Schultz had to find some of the three men's ex-lovers to interview. The producer wanted to see what they looked like after twenty years, and whether they still felt something for the men. Schultz was game, but when she called her editor at the newspaper and told him what she was doing, she found that he wasn't nearly as excited about it as she was. Schultz said that her editor had realized something she hadn't: that she was more involved in trying to solve the case than she was in writing articles about it. Schultz was enjoying being a detective a bit too much. Also, her editor told her, the case was decades old and only held so much interest for the public.

Still, Carol Schultz said in her book that she felt certain that having a segment about the North LaSalle Street murders on *Unsolved Mysteries* could bring out witnesses who had disappeared in the twenty years since the murders or who had been afraid to talk back then. So, in order to keep *Unsolved Mysteries* interested, Schultz began searching for some of the ex-lovers of Bob Gierse, Bob Hinson, and Jim Barker. The first woman she decided to go looking for was Gierse's girlfriend Diane

Horton. Schultz realized this would be no easy task after twenty years, and it wasn't; she later said it was only due to a chance meeting with Louise Cole, the former secretary for B&B Microfilming, that she was able to locate Diane Horton. In 1992, Cole was working as a receptionist at the Honda dealership where Schultz said she had her car serviced, and when she realized who Cole was, the reporter said she persuaded Cole to go to a local restaurant and talk.

According to Schultz, Cole told her that the murders had devastated her. She still thought about it, and told Schultz that she had cared so much for the three men that she would do whatever she could to help her solve their murders. So when Schultz told her about her quest to find Diane Horton, Cole told her that Diane's ex-husband, Carroll Horton, who owned an automobile parts and repair service, had called recently about doing business with the dealership where she worked. She said that she would call Carroll Horton and have him contact Schultz.

This would be the beginning of an almost four-year relationship between Carol Schultz and Carroll Horton. He would appear at first to want to help her in her investigation, encouraging her as she struggled to piece together the information she uncovered. Their relationship, however, would eventually take an extremely ugly turn.

CHAPTER SEVEN

In the spring of 1992, soon after asking Louise Cole to have Carroll Horton contact her, Carol Schultz received a telephone call from him. She said in her book that she told him that she was looking for the Diane Horton who had known the three men killed in the North LaSalle Street murders, and wondered if that was his ex-wife. The silence, Schultz said, stretched out for several seconds before he finally answered, yes, they had been divorced for a long time, but that they had been married once. Schultz then told him who she was and that she was writing about the North LaSalle Street murders. She knew that Diane Horton had been dating Bob Gierse at the time of his murder, and wasn't sure how cooperative her ex-husband would be, but she took a breath and then asked him if he would be willing to help her get in contact with Diane. Horton surprised her with his willingness to help, and told her that even though Diane had moved to Florida some time ago and they hadn't spoken in years, he would see if he could get a telephone number for her.

Horton then went on to tell Schultz about how the case had deeply affected his ex-wife, and about how emotionally distraught she had been for a long time afterward. The suddenness and savagery of the murders had crushed her. In truth, Horton said, he didn't believe his ex-wife had ever really gotten over it, and probably never would. Hearing this, Schultz felt that she had found a sympathetic ear, and so she decided to tell Horton the whole story about how she'd gotten interested in the case. She then went on to tell him about Margo and Michael Ray, and about how she'd identified the man with the strange eyes, who she believed had committed the murders.

Horton then surprised her by saying he had actually been inside the North LaSalle Street house on the day of the murders. He told her that he had seen the carnage firsthand, and he had seen the blood-soaked sheets covering the bodies. According to an article in *NUVO*, he claimed that he had been able to just walk past the police barrier, up onto the porch, where he said he told the officer guarding the door that he knew the three murdered men had been international spies. According to Horton, the officer, upon hearing this and apparently impressed, let him in to have a look around. How much of this tale Schultz believed is unclear, but although it was true that too many people trampled through the scene that day, they were nevertheless all police officers—no member of the general public would ever have been allowed inside (especially not one who was on the early suspect list like Carroll Horton, whose ex-wife was dating one of the victims). Regardless of what Horton told Schultz, homicide detectives don't allow sightseers into the crime scene. Homicide crime scenes are severely restricted areas, and anyone allowed into the crime scene is noted on the crime scene access list. Horton's story is not reflected in the official police reports or in the list of people who were allowed into the crime scene.

Perhaps the most inadvertently revealing thing Horton told Schultz was that he saw the bodies covered with sheets. The crime scene photos clearly show that the victims on North LaSalle Street certainly weren't. This is a Hollywood invention: In real life, homicide detectives don't cover murder victims with sheets, because a cover such as this could easily soak up any liquid evidence on the bodies and destroy it. The bodies are left just as they are found until they have been processed by the crime scene technicians and the coroner. And when the bodies are removed from the crime scene, they are usually put in body bags specifically built to retain evidence.

Carroll Horton *was* near the scene on that day, though. Still, "the closest Carroll Horton got to the crime scene was up to the crime scene barrier," said Michael Popcheff about Horton's claim. "I walked out and talked to him and told him I'd get with him later."

It seemed Horton wasn't one to let facts get in the way of a good story, however. According to Schultz's book, after he and Schultz had talked for a bit—and he had bragged to her that he had a photographic memory, had been awarded the Purple Heart in World War II, and possessed ESP—Horton suggested that they meet for dinner sometime to discuss the case. The two of them, he said, should pool their knowledge and talents. He told her that if they worked together she could probably win the Pulitzer Prize for her story. It's unclear how much of Horton's boasting Schultz believed at the time, but apparently she was compelled enough to feel flattered that he wanted to meet with her. After all, he could be of tremendous help to her research. He knew a lot about the victims, and he had been at the crime scene, maybe inside, maybe not, but still there. He had a lot of information she needed.

Ultimately, their relationship would very quickly become one of close confidants. Schultz, a single mother in her late twenties, worked closely with Horton, a gentleman in his midsixties who had been married seven times, on her story during the spring and summer of 1992. But while they would talk on the telephone about the North LaSalle Street case, they also soon became good friends and would share stories with each other about their lives. Schultz said in her book that she soon fell into the comfortable routine of calling Horton every day and talking. In her recollection of their relationship, she says that they talked on the telephone every day for six months, and occasionally more than once a day. He coined the pet name Pretty One for her. And yet, though they often talked as friends, Schultz also made sure that they always got back to the North LaSalle Street case. She had not lost a bit of her desire to solve it, and eventually decided that rather than a newspaper article she would write a book about the case.

Schultz apparently became so impressed by how much Horton knew about the North LaSalle Street murders that she said in an article in *NUVO* that she began to believe that perhaps he did have psychic powers after all. In her telephone conversations with Horton, she said Horton would tell her that he was going into a psychic trance and then, while in the trance, would claim he could see the murders on North LaSalle Street as they occurred. She said that he knew things about the murders that the police didn't (though how she verified this is uncertain).

But even though Horton assisted and encouraged her in her investigation, providing her with information from his psychic trances, Schultz knew that to solve the case she still had to find the man with the strange eyes. She now knew his name was Robert J. Leonard,[1] but she didn't know if he was alive or dead, and if alive, where he was living. He was the key. In her book about the case, Schultz says that she hired a professional bounty hunter she knew from having previously written newspaper articles about him. She wanted him to try to verify the location of Leonard, who Schultz had learned might now

---

[1] Denotes pseudonym

be living in Florida. She had gotten his name from the newspaper articles by Dick Cady and had used her news reporter investigative resources to find him. She wanted to be certain that he was still alive and living at the address she had. The bounty hunter, Schultz noted, apparently had to go to Florida anyway to locate a couple of bail skippers and so he agreed to take care of the matter for her while he was there.

Soon afterward, she got a call from the bounty hunter, who told her that he had located the man and had snapped some photographs of him for her. He still lived at the address she had for him. When Schultz called Horton to tell him about it, she waited as he went into a psychic trance. A few minutes later, he told her that she was right about this man being the killer. Schultz was thrilled. Although this didn't close the case, she now felt she had important information that eventually could.

Carroll Horton, though, did more than just encourage Schultz and go into psychic trances to verify her information. He also gave her the names of some people to contact about the case. He had been at the crime scene, his ex-wife had dated Gierse, and he knew a number of the principal people involved in the case. But his attempts to impress Schultz with his knowledge of the case would take a bad turn.

During the summer of 1992, Horton told Schultz that she needed to get ahold of a man who might know something about the murders, a dangerous criminal, he said, by the name of Floyd Chastain. Chastain had, in the 1970s, worked for Horton at his auto parts and repair shop, and he was now, Horton told her, currently serving a life sentence in Florida for murder.

By this time Schultz seemed to have become completely in awe of Horton. In addition to all of his other talents, he had bragged of having contacts in the criminal underworld. Horton had seemingly given her some pretty good information in the past, and so, thinking this seemed like a good idea, Carol Schultz wrote Floyd Chastain a letter that summer and said that she would like to speak with him about the North LaSalle Street murders. She told him she was writing a book about the crime and had heard that he might be able to help her. She gave Chastain a telephone number to call her at, but then, feeling the need to protect herself, she signed the letter using the pseudonym Betty Thompson.

When Schultz didn't hear anything from Chastain for several months, she forgot about the letter. But then, on September 1, 1992, Chastain called Schultz from the prison in Florida. At that time Schultz still worked for the *Indianapolis News*, and so they could patch Chastain's call from their office to her home telephone. Chastain told her that he knew a lot about the North LaSalle Street murders, things no one else knew, and that he also knew who the murderer on North LaSalle Street had been. Schultz, flustered but impressed, told him about her research and about how she had found Leonard living in Florida. She told Chastain that she felt certain Leonard had been the North LaSalle Street killer. Chastain, though, told her that she had it wrong, that the killer wasn't that man, but that he knew who the real killer was.

According to *NUVO*, Chastain told Schultz, "Ma'am, I know the man who killed the men on LaSalle. If you come down here, I'll tell you."

Having a young son to take care of, Schultz knew she couldn't make the thousand-mile trip to Florida, so she tried to get Chastain to tell her who the killer was. But when he wouldn't tell her, she began guessing. She asked if the killer was still alive, and Chastain said yes. After some more questions from Schultz, Chastain also told her that the North LaSalle Street killer still lived in Indianapolis. Schultz then tried to guess the killer's occupation. Finally, after a number of wrong guesses, she asked Chastain if the murderer worked in the car business. When Chastain said yes, Schultz said that she thought about it for a moment and then asked him if the murderer on North LaSalle Street had been Carroll Horton. Chastain said yes, Carroll Horton was the killer. Chastain told her that he had watched Horton slice Gierse's throat with a knife.

According to Schultz, Chastain told her that he had been with Horton at North LaSalle Street on the night of the murders. Chastain claimed to her that he had just been the getaway driver, though eventually this story would change several times. He then told her that the sentence he was serving right then in Florida was for another murder that Horton had committed, but which he had taken the fall for. He claimed that Horton had beaten a man to death with a board and then promised to do things for Chastain if he took the rap. Chastain said he was scared to say no. Chastain also told Schultz that Horton was a serial killer who had claimed victims all over the United States.

One question that never seemed to have occurred to Carol Schultz during her investigation was that if Horton and Chastain had really been murder coconspirators on North LaSalle Street, why would Horton have introduced her to Chastain? Why would a man who had been working very hard to impress her then put Schultz in contact with someone who knew incriminating things about him?

Also, in Schultz's recounting of her telephone conversation that day with Chastain, she doesn't offer any information or evidence as to why she believed a voice on a telephone. She doesn't tell what made her, an investigative reporter, believe the story of a man she knew was serving a life sentence for murder, a man she had never met and knew practically nothing about. But nevertheless, she *did* believe Chastain and became absolutely certain from that point on that Horton was not just the North LaSalle Street murderer, but also a serial killer who had claimed victims all over the United States. Schultz said that following this initial telephone call, Chastain called her several more times that month with more information about Horton and his crimes. After this, she said, they began to talk regularly, usually every Saturday afternoon.

Following her initial conversation with Floyd Chastain, Carol Schultz said in her book that she spent the rest of the day in terror, fearing that at any minute Carroll Horton would be at her door, ready to make her his next victim. (Why she thought Horton would know about what Chastain had told her was unclear, but she apparently felt certain that he did, and it terrified her.) Schultz recounts how sometime later she called a retired police officer she knew, who came to her house. After listening to her story and a tape of her conversation with Chastain, she said he advised her to get a gun and learn how to use it.

Schultz also said that, following Chastain's bombshell, she felt the need to test Horton. So she called him and made up a story about having evidence that a man who went by the name of Fat Alex had committed the North LaSalle Street murders. Schultz said she then asked Horton to use his ESP powers and see if this was true. According to Schultz, Horton acted as though he was going into a psychic trance and finally told her that, yes, she was right; Fat Alex had committed the murders. Schultz said she knew right then that Horton was the murderer and that he'd only been stringing her along with his offers of help in her investigation. The perhaps likelier motive she apparently didn't consider was that Carroll Horton was an elderly man who was infatuated by a beautiful young woman and was telling her whatever it was he thought she wanted to hear.

Eventually, Carol Schultz told Lieutenant Michael Popcheff about what she had found out in her conversations with Floyd Chastain. While she claimed that Popcheff didn't seem impressed or enthusiastic about what she had found, police department records show that on September 14, 1992, Popcheff had the Identification

Branch at the police department compare Carroll Horton's fingerprints with the still unidentified fingerprints from North LaSalle Street. They didn't match.

A week after her initial telephone conversation with Chastain, in which he had fingered Horton as the North LaSalle Street killer, Schultz went to the Prosecutor's Office. She brought with her the tape of her conversation with Chastain. She said she felt certain that the prosecutor would immediately issue an arrest warrant for Horton. The case, she imagined, would be solved and closed. She would write the book. It would be a bestseller.

However, things didn't turn out that way.

For someone like Carol Schultz, who had never dealt with criminals on a daily basis, and didn't know how they will lie to get something they want, will lie to get themselves out of trouble, and sometimes will lie simply because that is their lifestyle, the tape she had brought along seemed damning. Apparently, it didn't occur to her that Floyd Chastain might be lying; that he, like Carroll Horton, might be simply trying to impress her. The prosecutor, however, wasn't impressed by the tape.

A prosecutor has to have a lot more evidence than just a taped conversation with a man that neither the prosecutor nor Schultz knew anything about before a murder warrant could be issued. A successful prosecution for murder took much more. Consequently, the prosecutor told Schultz that nothing could be done with just the evidence she had. Also, the prosecutor knew that an arrest for murder could ruin a person's life, and, even if dropped later, would still follow that person forever. It was no small accusation to make.

In the book she wrote about her investigation, Schultz said that she could not understand why the prosecutor wouldn't take the information she had and immediately go out and arrest Horton. She said she was flabbergasted and left the office bitterly disappointed. What did they want? She had proof! And as if her rejection by the prosecutor wasn't bad enough, she also found out that the *Unsolved Mysteries* story had apparently fallen through.

Schultz, however, refused to give up and became determined to gather enough evidence so that the prosecutor would have to arrest Horton. To this end, she eventually contacted Horton's ex-wife Diane in Florida. When Schultz told Diane she wanted to speak with her about Bob Gierse, she said Diane began crying. Schultz also claimed that when she asked Diane if she thought her husband might have been the killer on North LaSalle Street, Diane told her after a few moments that she didn't know. To Schultz this seemed like just a little more confirmation.

During Schultz's attempts to gather evidence on Horton, she also arranged for Floyd Chastain and Carroll Horton to talk with her in a three-way telephone call, hoping that during it Horton would confess or at least be forced into saying something incriminating. During the conversations, though, Horton gave Schultz nothing she could use, but he did become (understandably) very upset during these exchanges, especially when Chastain attempted to accuse him of being involved in the North

LaSalle Street murders and a number of other crimes. Horton called Chastain a liar, and was almost certainly regretting his decision to put Schultz in contact with him.

Interestingly enough, even after Chastain had told Schultz that Horton had committed the murders on North LaSalle Street, which she apparently believed, Schultz still continued to call and talk with Horton every day. She said that she only called him because she was afraid that if she stopped, he would become suspicious that she believed Chastain's story that he was a killer. She didn't want to be his next victim, so she religiously called him every morning between 5:30 and 6:00 A.M. to catch him before he went to work.

Finally, unwilling to give up in her attempt to gather evidence against Horton, Schultz said that she decided to go out on a date with him and try to get him to make an incriminating statement, a statement that would be enough that the prosecutor would have to arrest him. To this end, she called and asked Horton to dinner, and also arranged for her bounty hunter friend to sit out in the parking lot just in case. At dinner, though, all Horton talked about was himself and his exploits during World War II. She tried over and over to guide the conversation back to the North LaSalle Street murders, but Horton was uninterested in the topic and would go right back to talking about himself.

The day following their dinner, Schultz said, Horton called her and told her how pretty she was, and how someone could very easily fall in love with her. She said that a long silence followed this statement, as though he was waiting for the appropriate reply. Schultz said she realized right then that Horton had fallen in love with her. She felt thunderstruck and didn't know what to say in response. And so she got off of the telephone as quickly as possible.

But Carroll Horton wasn't the only one in love with Carol Schultz. While Schultz spoke with Horton on the telephone every day, she also talked regularly on the telephone with Floyd Chastain. According to Chastain, she also sent him information about the North LaSalle Street murders, though it is never explained why she did this since Chastain claimed to have been there. It's also not clear what the two of them talked about on the telephone, but whatever it was apparently made Chastain fall in love. He reportedly even sent her a ring from prison. In later correspondence with detectives at the Indianapolis Police Department, Chastain claimed the feelings were mutual, and that he and Schultz were in love.

However, for Schultz, while she might have felt safe from Chastain, who was safely locked away in a prison in Florida, the thought of Horton being in love with her terrified her. Since she believed him to be a serial killer, she continued to fear that his next victim might well be her. He lived much too close, and she was much too vulnerable, especially if he found out what she believed about him. Schultz finally decided that she couldn't just live in constant fear. She had to do something about it, and what she decided to do was to contact Joe McAtee, the detective lieutenant who in 1971 had been in charge of the North LaSalle Street murder investigation.

Joe McAtee had been a rising star at the Indianapolis Police Department through the 1970s and '80s. Following his stint as a detective lieutenant in the Homicide Branch, McAtee had been promoted to captain, then deputy chief of operations, and finally to chief of police, a position he held for five years. Not satisfied, however, with just being the chief of police, McAtee then ran for and easily won election to become the sheriff of Marion County, which was the office he held when Schultz called him in late 1992 to request an appointment.

Schultz said that she felt very intimidated meeting Sheriff McAtee and wasn't certain he would believe her. However, she convinced him to listen as she played him one of the tape recordings she had made. According to Schultz, after listening to it, McAtee then called Lieutenant Popcheff and told him that they needed to meet right away. Schultz said she felt elated. She had finally gotten someone in authority to listen to her. Sheriff McAtee was going to reopen the North LaSalle Street case.

CHAPTER EIGHT

Following Carol Schultz's meeting with Sheriff Joe McAtee, the Marion County Sheriff's Office began looking into her claim of knowing who the killer on North LaSalle Street had been. The sheriff immediately began having meetings with Lieutenant Michael Popcheff, apparently to map out their strategy.

There was apparently some discussion within the Prosecutor's Office about the sheriff looking into a crime more than two decades old that didn't seem to fall within his jurisdiction. At this time, the sheriff's responsibilities didn't include crime inside the old city limits (which would include the North LaSalle Street address). McAtee responded in an article in *NUVO*, "No one can tell me I can't investigate crime inside Marion County. And if I don't do it, it won't get done." Like the other original detectives on the North LaSalle Street case, he wanted to see it solved.

As Schultz waited for something to happen on that end, she also decided to do something herself to help move the investigation along. If she was going to write the book, she figured that she needed to take an active part in solving the case. So she came up with a new idea of how to gather evidence against Carroll Horton that the police could use. She decided she would go to dinner with Horton again, but this time, rather than a tape recorder in her purse, she would be wearing a concealed microphone that the police could listen in on. She would try to get him to make some incriminating statements or maybe even a confession if she was lucky. Eventually, he would have to say something that would prove he was the killer, and with the police listening to the conversation they could step in and make an arrest just as soon as he had said enough.

Schultz said she called the sheriff and proposed her idea to him. Sheriff McAtee apparently liked the idea—she claims he even offered to provide her with a body wire to wear under her clothing and told her that he would have some of his officers stationed nearby using surveillance equipment. They would listen in on the dinner meeting, and if she could get Horton to say anything incriminating, they would be able to record it. Schultz admitted she felt a bit guilty about what she was doing, since she knew that Horton had fallen in love with her, and that she was going to use this fact to get him to incriminate himself. But still, she felt justified because she truly believed that Horton was a serial killer who ought to be brought to justice.

On the night of the dinner date, Schultz said, a female deputy came to her house with the body wire. As she got dressed for her date with Horton, the deputy fastened the recording device to her. Schultz was all set to go catch a murderer.

As she had planned, Schultz and Horton were to meet for dinner at Mickler's Sirloin Inn on the east side of Indianapolis. Schultz arrived early at the restaurant, and first went to talk with the sheriff, who was sitting in the back of a surveillance van parked at the rear of the parking lot. She said that Sheriff McAtee told her she needed to try to get Horton to talk about being inside the North LaSalle Street house on the day of the murders. Although Horton had claimed to her that he'd been inside the house and had viewed the crime scene, the sheriff told her that Horton had definitely not been allowed inside the house on the day the murders were discovered, so any information he had about the crime scene (the positions of the bodies, the condition of the house, etc.) could be incriminating.

Schultz said in her book that she had once again brought along her bounty hunter friend that night, just in case she needed help right away. Even though sheriff's deputies sat out in the parking lot, she wanted someone much closer. The bounty hunter agreed to sit at a nearby table, and would pretend to eat alone, while all the time waiting to jump in if she needed him. Schultz went into the restaurant, was seated, and then waited for Horton.

When he was late arriving, Schultz began to worry that perhaps he was on to her and knew what she was doing. Panic set in momentarily until Horton finally walked in the door and apologized for being late, explaining that an emergency at work had held him up.

Schultz smiled and tried to act as though it was nothing at all. They ordered their dinners, but just like the previous time, although during the meal Schultz tried to get Horton to talk about the North LaSalle Street murders, he instead talked about everything else. He did tell her, though, about going to his ex-wife's apartment one time to pick up his children and seeing Gierse run out the back door carrying his pants. He also told her about the top secret documents Gierse and Hinson were supposedly working on, the same information he said he had given to the police at the murder scene. Yet, while he didn't give Schultz any incriminating information, Horton did try to get her to come and spend the night with him at his place. He told her to pack a toothbrush and her pajamas and meet him there. She politely declined, and then began to worry again that he was on to her and that was why she couldn't get him to say anything incriminating. Did he know what she was up to?

Schultz said that when she realized she wasn't going to get any incriminating evidence she told Horton she had to leave. She got up and hurried out, terrified that Horton would follow her. She knew she had to get out of there. She didn't want to be the next victim of a serial killer. According to her recollections, she got into her car, pulled out of the parking lot, and then drove to a drive-in restaurant nearby where she had made plans to meet with the bounty hunter after the dinner. Minutes later, the bounty hunter pulled into the parking lot and she got out of her car and into his. They pulled out, leaving her car there.

Schultz said she finally felt safe. But it was short-lived. Once in the car the bounty hunter told her that he had spotted a member of the Mafia sitting at a table near her, and that the man had watched her conversation with Horton intently. How the bounty hunter would have known the man was a Mafia member wasn't explained (and even more puzzling given that those individuals seldom found their way to Indianapolis). But the bounty hunter wasn't finished with his revelations. Schultz said he told her that they were being followed at the moment, probably by the Mafia, and for her to hang on and he would lose them. He then floored the accelerator.

Naturally, the police—who were unaware of Schultz's backup plans with the bounty hunter—were concerned about her sudden disappearance. Popcheff, who had joined the sheriff's deputies in the surveillance van, said that halfway through the meal with Horton the body wire suddenly shut off and Schultz disappeared. Concerned for her safety, the police went looking for Schultz and finally found her at her house. Popcheff said she told them that she had become frightened and that was why she left abruptly.

Sheriff McAtee, according to Schultz, was disappointed that Horton hadn't said anything incriminating during the dinner date and, like Schultz before, apparently had no luck trying to persuade the Prosecutor's Office to go after Horton. So finally, Schultz said she decided to try the direct approach. She would confront Horton with her belief that he was the killer on North LaSalle Street and force him into an incriminating statement. She had been talking with Horton now every day for over a year, and so, in one of their telephone calls, Schultz told Horton that Chastain had fingered him to the police, and that, because of this, he was now their number one suspect in the North LaSalle Street murders. She said that Horton flew into a rage and called Chastain a liar. He also complained to her that he would now be forced to hire an attorney. However, to her dismay, he didn't say anything incriminating.

Horton told her he believed Chastain had actually been the killer on North LaSalle Street. While she didn't contradict him, she didn't believe it, either. She still believed Chastain's story that it was Horton. Schultz said that as she continued to talk with Horton every day on the telephone, however, she quickly discovered that he was jealous of the time she spent with Lieutenant Popcheff and would constantly try to belittle him. Horton thought that Popcheff had romantic ideas about her, which she said was ridiculous. He was a perfect gentleman.

Schultz, along with talking daily to Horton, was also continuing to speak regularly with Chastain every Saturday afternoon, long-distance from his prison in Florida. During these conversations, Chastain continued to implicate Horton in more and more crimes. He told Schultz that Horton had bragged to him about killing a young girl named Connie and burying her body at his house. Chastain also claimed that he knew about another murder Horton had committed, this one of an elderly woman. Chastain told Schultz that she ought to have the police get a search warrant and dig up Horton's property. He bet they'd turn up a lot of bodies.

However, a little later in Schultz's investigation, a columnist for the *Indianapolis Star* wrote that he had talked to two acquaintances of Chastain, and they both said that Chastain had a habit of telling tall tales. One of the acquaintances also claimed that Chastain had once abducted and tried to rape her. Another said that Chastain, after making his accusations of murder against Horton, had then tried to shake Horton down for $50,000 from prison. Chastain allegedly said that for $50,000 he would tell the authorities he had lied and that Horton really wasn't involved in the North LaSalle Street murders.

Carol Schultz had been very happy when Sheriff McAtee took an active interest in her claims, and although Lieutenant Popcheff had earlier only assisted her in an advisory capacity, meeting and talking with her at the Waffle House, he eventually joined forces with McAtee to investigate her claims about Horton and the North LaSalle Street murders. One day, she said, Popcheff even took her to the police department property room and allowed her to see and smell the bloody clothing worn by Gierse and Hinson. She said it repulsed her, but when she recounted the experience to her bounty hunter friend, he told her that it was a shame they didn't have the investigative technology then that they have today. He told her they could probably have solved the case right away. This started Schultz thinking about whether these same scientific advances could still be used on the case. After conferring with a friend about this, Schultz contacted the very prestigious Vidocq Society.

This organization, based in Philadelphia, is made up of former homicide detectives, forensic scientists, medical examiners, and others involved in homicide investigation. This group will lend assistance to police departments and other organizations involved in extremely difficult murder investigations, and particularly in cold cases (murder cases that have been inactivated and shelved because of a lack of evidence or witnesses). The group sent an investigator to Indianapolis, who conferred with the sheriff and took a look at the evidence. After this, he flew back to Philadelphia to present the case to the society. Because only a few cases the society sees every year actually have a chance of solution, and because the cost of an investigation is so high, the society typically declines most of the cases presented to it. However, the society voted to look into the North LaSalle Street case and lend Carol Schultz a hand. The society would later question whether this had been a good decision.

According to an article in the September 1996 issue of *Indianapolis Monthly* magazine, several members of the society said they didn't know when they accepted the case how emotionally involved Carol Schultz was in the investigation. They soon found out, however. These members said that they continuously warned Schultz that she needed to distance herself from the case, but apparently she couldn't. Consequently, the members soon began feeling very uncomfortable about the investigation. According to the magazine article, one of the members said, "Dealing with her is like trying to herd a group of cats down a driveway." Nevertheless, despite their doubts, several members of the society came to Indianapolis to investigate. Alas, however, though they looked at all aspects of the case, they were unable to come up with much more than the police already had.

Meanwhile, because of the information Carol Schultz had supplied, Sheriff Joe McAtee, Lieutenant Michael Popcheff, and Jim Strode (by then retired) flew to Florida and spoke with Floyd Chastain. They apparently believed that Carol Schultz had uncovered clues they had missed in 1971. The men returned cautious, but encouraged. They didn't know at that time, however, how much of the information Chastain had given them he had gotten from Carol Schultz in the first place.

Eventually, two other detectives, Lieutenant Charles Briley and Lieutenant Louis Christ (who would later become the deputy chief of investigations), also traveled to Florida to follow up on the earlier questioning of Chastain. They weren't nearly as impressed.

"We interviewed Chastain twice and we couldn't decide if he was telling us the truth or not," said Briley. So he decided to try a new tactic. "When we interviewed Chastain a third time, I told my partner that I was going to tell him some silly things, and to just go along with whatever I said. So I told Chastain some things about the crime scene that weren't true, and I found that they would become a part of his story. This proved to me that he wasn't there. For example, I mentioned a vacant lot next door to the crime scene, and he said, 'Yeah, that's where we parked.' There was no vacant lot next door."

Lieutenant Christ agreed with Briley's assessment. "Floyd Chastain made up everything he said about that case," said Christ. "He had no direct knowledge of any of that. There was nothing he said that he could substantiate."

At the conclusion of his interviews, Chastain apparently realized that Briley and Christ knew he was lying, and he panicked. Lying to police officers or prison officials is a violation that can result in a revocation of privileges. "The last thing Chastain said to us was 'Please don't tell the warden that I lied,'" said Christ. "He knew he was going to lose all of his phone privileges. The guy had absolutely nothing of his own as far as knowledge of that crime."

Eventually, though, another person who claimed to know something about the North LaSalle Street murders also surfaced. On March 9, 1993, at around 5:30 P.M., the Indianapolis Police Department received a call from a woman named Mary Cavanaugh.[1] Cavanaugh said she wanted to report an attempted burglary at her house.

Officer Tony Lorenzano arrived to take the report and

---

[1] Denotes pseudonym

discovered that someone had definitely tried to get in. He found pry marks and fresh wood chips at her side door, but also found that entry hadn't been gained and nothing had been taken. As is standard police procedure, he explained to Cavanaugh that he would make a report and try to keep an eye on her house, and then he started to leave. However, as he did so, Lorenzano said Cavanaugh suddenly became very upset and started asking him what he knew about the North LaSalle Street murders. She claimed that she had recently been in contact with Sheriff McAtee about it. Cavanaugh then also told Officer Lorenzano that a man named Carroll Horton had been trying to contact her through her daughter. Cavanaugh said she hadn't heard from Horton in over twenty years.

Cavanaugh then began telling Officer Lorenzano about being at the North LaSalle Street house on the night of the murders. She told him that when she walked into the house there was blood everywhere, that two of the men were already dead, and that they were getting ready to kill the third, who was begging for his life. She said she started screaming, and Carroll Horton, who was supervising the murders, slapped her and told her to shut up. She claimed that Horton then made her go to a typewriter in the house and type a message that said, "This is what happens to people who cross me." (There is no mention in the original 1971 homicide case file of there even having been a typewriter in the house on North LaSalle Street, let alone of the police finding any note such as the one Cavanaugh claimed she typed.)

Although Officer Lorenzano hadn't been a member of the police department when the North LaSalle Street murders occurred, he clearly still knew about them. So he immediately contacted the Marion County Sheriff's Office in an attempt to verify that Cavanaugh had spoken with Sheriff McAtee about the case. He wasn't able to raise anyone at the Sheriff's Homicide Office but did finally manage to get ahold of one of their homicide run cars. The deputy in the run car said that he had heard that McAtee, Popcheff, and Strode had flown down to Florida recently to talk with a man in prison there about the North LaSalle Street killings, but that was all he knew about it.

Officer Lorenzano then called Lieutenant Popcheff at home. When he told him what Cavanaugh had said, Popcheff told Lorenzano that he would be there as soon as he could. Within thirty minutes, both McAtee and Popcheff had arrived at Cavanaugh's home and had taken over.

Unfortunately, what McAtee and Popcheff apparently didn't know was that Carol Schultz would also soon be in contact with Mary Cavanaugh and her family, and possibly taint anything Cavanaugh would tell the police. Schultz said in her book that Sheriff McAtee called and told her about Mary Cavanaugh. Schultz somehow obtained Cavanaugh's unlisted telephone number and called her. Although Cavanaugh wouldn't talk with Schultz and told her to never call her back, Schultz talked to Cavanaugh's daughter, and told her about the murders. Schultz gave her some pictures of the North LaSalle Street victims and asked her to show them to her mother and see if they stirred up any memories. When Cavanaugh's daughter showed her mother the photographs, she said her mother didn't show any signs of recognition, and indeed said that she didn't know the men. Only later did she seem to start remembering things.

Since Mary Cavanaugh had made some very damning statements against Carroll Horton, however, the police department realized that they needed to investigate whether or not Cavanaugh was a reliable witness. They assigned this task to Detective Sergeant Don Wright. On March 30, 1993, about three weeks after the initial break-in call, Detective Wright wrote a memo about the various interviews he had conducted concerning Cavanaugh. He said he met first with a man named Sam Gibson, who had lived with Cavanaugh from 1976 to 1987. Gibson said that Cavanaugh had a serious drinking problem the whole time they had been together. But he also said that she had never once during the time he knew her mentioned the North LaSalle Street murders. Gibson added that in 1978 or 1979 Cavanaugh introduced him to Carroll Horton, who she said was an excellent mechanic. She didn't seem frightened or intimidated by him, and in fact Gibson told Wright that Cavanaugh and Horton appeared to be very good friends, and that he suspected they might have been even closer than that.

Gibson then told Wright about how in the early part of 1993, long after he and Cavanaugh had parted ways, he saw Horton come into a bar he was in. He said he watched Horton walk over and ask the bartender for information about Cavanaugh, specifically her address. The bartender couldn't help him, but Gibson said he stopped Horton and told him that he could get Cavanaugh's telephone number for him, which he did.

Although Horton originally told Gibson that he needed to talk to Cavanaugh about some tax problems he was having with a house he had bought from her, Gibson said that Horton later told him he really needed to contact her because Floyd Chastain was trying to pin some murders on him, and he needed to talk to her about it.

Detective Sergeant Wright, in his report, also mentioned speaking with a man named Bert Cavanaugh,[2] Mary Cavanaugh's first husband. Like Gibson, he said that Mary had never once mentioned anything to him about the North LaSalle Street murders during the time they were together.

Lieutenants Louis Christ and Charles Briley also assisted in attempting to verify Cavanaugh's reliability as a witness. They weren't impressed with what they turned up.

"Mary Cavanaugh's memory was so bad that she couldn't even tell us where she used to live," said Christ. "We drove her down there and she let us drive right past her old house. She had no idea where it was."

The Prosecutor's Office wasn't impressed with Mary Cavanaugh's recollections, either. There were far too many inconsistencies, enough to make them very wary

---

[2] Denotes pseudonym

of issuing a murder warrant based on them. Also, they worried about reports that she had a serious drinking problem, which they feared would further damage her credibility if the case went to court.

On November 3, 1993, the Identification Branch of the Indianapolis Police Department said that Cavanaugh's fingerprints didn't match any of the unidentified fingerprints the crime lab technicians had found in the house.

Still, despite the reluctance of the Prosecutor's Office to issue a murder warrant, the Indianapolis Police Department—because of the information supplied by Carol Schultz, Floyd Chastain, and Mary Cavanaugh—did decide to officially reopen the North LaSalle Street case. The police department felt that they needed to take a fresh look at the case, so veteran homicide detective Jon Layton was assigned to head up the reopened investigation.

Layton, of course, had to start from the beginning and read the entire 1971 case file. Then he had to look at what Carol Schultz claimed were fresh leads that would solve the case once and for all.

CHAPTER NINE

On April 11, 1994, Indianapolis homicide detective Jon Layton, after reading through the 1971 homicide case file and reviewing the recent statements from Carol Schultz, Floyd Chastain, and Mary Cavanaugh, typed up a probable cause affidavit and submitted it to the Prosecutor's Office. A probable cause affidavit basically tells the prosecutor what evidence a detective has in a case, listing the witnesses and what they said. It also details the physical evidence available, which can not only support what the witnesses said, but also tie a suspect to the crime. In addition, it contains any other information available that the detective feels can support his or her assertion that a certain person committed a crime. The prosecutor, after reading the probable cause affidavit, can then decide whether or not to issue arrest warrants based on this information and evidence.

In the case of the North LaSalle Street murders, the prosecutor declined. No arrest warrants would be issued based just on what evidence Layton had available, which was mostly witness statements with really no new hard physical evidence. Most prosecutors, besides not wanting to damage someone's reputation by arresting him or her for a murder that can't be proved, and through this waste taxpayer money, also live and die by their conviction rate. Every prosecutor wants to brag about having a high conviction rate. It's how they measure their success. Also, few individuals who run for the office of prosecutor see it as an end. Most see it as a springboard to a higher political office. But to get to this higher office they have to have been successful as a prosecutor. Therefore, taking on a case that has a strong likelihood of falling apart in court is never an attractive idea.

In addition, in any murder investigation, while it is nice to have statements from witnesses, and even confessions, these cannot take the place of hard evidence. Jurors like to see physical evidence that can tie a suspect to a crime. Jurors like to see fingerprints or DNA left behind at the crime scene. Jurors like to have the murder weapon found in the suspect's possession or the victim's blood on the suspect's clothing. Members of a jury feel much more comfortable about convicting someone when there is physical evidence. Jurors don't like to convict on murder charges—which typically carry a lengthy prison sentence or even the death penalty—unless they can see convincing evidence the person is guilty. In the North LaSalle Street case, however, no physical evidence at all tied Carroll Horton to the murders. All the police had were the statements supplied by Floyd Chastain, a convicted felon, and Mary Cavanaugh, an apparently unreliable witness.

This is not to say that witness statements have no prosecutorial value. They do. But prosecutors know that statements can often be distorted by what a witness has read somewhere, has heard from other witnesses, or believes he or she saw based on the witness's opinion of the perpetrator. How a person feels about someone else can often color their impressions of what they see. For example, acts that would appear innocuous when done by ordinary people can often appear devious and criminal if done by someone a witness doesn't like.

Also, prosecutors must always consider whether witnesses may be lying for some reason. The witness may actually be the perpetrator and is trying to shift the blame, or the witness may have a grudge against someone and is lying as payback. In addition to this, people simply see events differently. Ask any police officer taking witness statements at the scene of a crime: It can be amazing how differently people who witnessed the same event saw it. That's why statements like these have to be confirmed or corroborated by physical evidence in order to carry real evidentiary weight.

In the case of Mary Cavanaugh, the prosecutor saw serious problems. When Cavanaugh told the police that she had been dragged into the murder scene, she was talking about events that had occurred well over twenty years earlier, and which had been reported on extensively in the news media. The prosecutor knew that Cavanaugh had very likely read and heard a lot about the North La-Salle Street murders over the passing years. Anyone living in Indianapolis during that time couldn't help but hear about them. Also, the prosecutor was concerned about reports of a drinking problem, which raised fears about how this condition could affect her memory.

Additionally, the police had had Cavanaugh hypnotized in an attempt to enhance her memory. While this technique can assist people in recalling traumatic events, it is also fraught with problems. Individuals in a hypnotic state are very prone to suggestion and can be made to "remember" events that are suggested to them. Consequently, the prosecutor knew that a good defense attorney would jump all over the issue of Mary Cavanaugh having been hypnotized, using it as evidence that her testimony was unreliable.

But Cavanaugh wasn't the only witness that the prosecutor had trouble with. Carol Schultz admitted that she'd told Chastain details from the case files, such as the fact that there had been pizza boxes under the coffee table in the living room of the North LaSalle Street house (something Chastain had related back to the police to convince them he had been there). She also admitted to sending him a newspaper clipping, the contents of which, like the pizza boxes, Chastain had used in his statements to the police. Schultz later agreed that she told Chastain too much about the case, rather than letting him tell her. Schultz apparently didn't realize that, like Horton, Chastain had fallen in love with her and wanted very much to impress her. He obviously believed that having and sharing knowledge about the North La-Salle Street murderers was the way to do it.

Between the lack of physical evidence and the issues with Chastain and Cavanaugh, the prosecutor simply didn't think that the police had enough evidence to warrant an arrest. He felt they simply had no chance of winning with just what they had, so he declined to act.

Carol Schultz said in her book that she again felt devastated that the Prosecutor's Office wouldn't do anything. She had been positive that with Layton taking over the case, and with Cavanaugh adding her testimony to Chastain's, it would be more than enough. Schultz's take on this latest setback was that she'd heard the prosecutor, because of an upcoming election, didn't want to do anything that could turn out badly (which this case had the strong possibility of doing). She said she felt crushed.

Despite being deeply disappointed by the prosecutor's decision, Carol Schultz continued to stay in constant contact with both Carroll Horton and Floyd Chastain. She simply could not give up hope of eventually bringing Horton to justice. And the book, she knew, wouldn't have a proper ending without an arrest and trial.

Then, according to Schultz, a new wrinkle in the case appeared. Early one morning Chastain called her collect from the prison in Florida. She said he told her that he had been up all night praying and that he had something he wanted to confess to her.

Chastain had earlier told Schultz that he had just

been the driver of the getaway car, and that was his total involvement in the North LaSalle Street murders. But now he told her that this wasn't true. He was actually much more involved than that. Chastain's new story was that on the morning of December 1, 1971, he drove his mother's car to the North LaSalle Street address. In the car with him, Chastain said, were Carroll Horton and a man named Michael Golden,[1] or as Chastain knew him, "Big Mike." Chastain said that he parked the car and went into the house with them and, while they were there, two *other* men, named Paul Green[2] and Ben Wheeler,[3] drove up in an El Camino, and they also came into the house. A little later, a woman in a black Cadillac pulled up in front. According to Chastain, Horton went out and brought the woman inside. (Including the three victims, this now placed nine people in the house.)

Chastain told Schultz that he witnessed Horton slice Bob Gierse's throat, and next watched Big Mike kill Jim Barker. Chastain said that Horton then ordered him to either slit Bob Hinson's throat or else they would kill him. So he did it. He said he later went outside and threw up.

Schultz said in her book that, after this confession, Chastain began talking about all of Horton's other victims, naming almost a dozen, until the operator finally

---

[1] Denotes pseudonym

[2] Denotes pseudonym

[3] Denotes pseudonym

cut him off. (The Indianapolis Police Department Identification Branch would later compare the fingerprints of
all of the individuals identified by Chastain as taking part
in the North LaSalle Street murders, including Chastain's, with the still unidentified fingerprints found inside the North LaSalle Street house. No matches were
found.)

Later on, after digesting all of this information, and
feeling it to be even more of a justification for her belief
about the North LaSalle Street murders, Schultz tried to
call Horton and found to her surprise that the phone
service for the number she used to reach him at his shop
had been disconnected. She checked and found that in
fact all of the telephone lines going into his shop had
been disconnected. She began panicking. Something was
wrong. Did Horton know how much she knew about his
involvement in the murders? The panic really took hold
after she next called the electric and gas companies and
found that their services were also being disconnected.
Later that night, when Chastain called her collect again,
Schultz told him about Horton disappearing. Chastain
said he thought that Horton was probably trying to flee
the country, and he again urged her to try to get the
police to search Horton's property for bodies.

When Schultz finally did make contact with Horton
the next day at noon, she said she screamed at him for
not letting her know that he was having his telephone
service disconnected. He explained the disconnections
by telling her about his need to downsize his auto business and move everything into just one building. Schultz

finally calmed down and then they talked for a while. Following this, she and Horton then returned to their daily telephone calls.

Despite Carol Schultz's continued contact with Horton and Chastain following the prosecutor's refusal to proceed, nothing was happening in the North LaSalle Street case. It simply sat dormant, as it had for well over twenty years. Schultz knew that something had to be done. So she decided that perhaps a little more publicity could stir things up a bit. She contacted *NUVO,* the largest alternative newspaper in Indianapolis, and persuaded them to commit to publishing an article concerning what she had uncovered about the North LaSalle Street murders.

Schultz said that when she told Carroll Horton about the article she was going to write for *NUVO,* he seemed very pleased. He told her that she needed all the publicity she could get if she wanted the book she was writing to be a success. According to Schultz, he then asked her if she was worried about him going to jail, and she told him yes. She later said that she couldn't believe her attachment to him. She wrote that even though she honestly believed Horton to be a murderer, she still felt sorry for him.

But Schultz also feared him. She still believed him to be a serial killer who wouldn't hesitate to add her to his list of victims. Although Sheriff McAtee didn't recall this, she said she mentioned to him how scared she was of Horton, and McAtee, she said, sympathized with her and offered to park an empty sheriff's car out in front of her house. (With it out front, the thinking went, if Horton passed by he would believe a deputy was inside.) She said McAtee told her she'd have to occasionally move the car and park it in different positions so that Horton would think the deputy had left and then came back.

Sometime earlier, in late 1993, Schultz had resigned from her job as a reporter for the *Indianapolis News*. She knew she had to. Schultz said her editor told her that she had gotten much too close to the police in her investigation of the North LaSalle Street killings. He told her that a reporter didn't do undercover work for the police. Her going to dinner wearing a body wire that the police could listen in on had compromised her ethics. Journalists simply didn't do that.

Consequently, on New Year's Eve 1993, as Schultz sat at home, lonely and depressed, waiting for 1994, she said she wished she had someone to share it with, but that she hadn't dated much since she started the North LaSalle Street investigation. It had taken over her life. Finally, bored with being alone, she decided to call Horton. He told her that she shouldn't be alone on New Year's Eve, but out celebrating with someone. He then suggested that she come over to his place for the night, but she turned him down. Instead, she plugged in the tape recorder and tried to get him to talk about the North LaSalle Street killings. They talked for three hours, but still no confession or incriminating statements.

Horton, however, did reportedly tell her that Sheriff McAtee had asked him to come down and take a lie detector test, but that his attorney had told him not to.

Horton, though, said he was considering it. He said he was innocent, and that taking a lie detector test might be the best thing to do since it would prove he was innocent.

Horton eventually did show up for a lie detector test, but then apparently decided at the last moment that it wouldn't be in his best interests to go through with it after all.

"We had Carroll Horton in for a lie detector test," confirmed Popcheff. "When he arrived, he asked if we had a doctor or a hospital close by, and all of a sudden he's having heart problems. He never did take a lie detector test."

Regardless though of Horton's decision not to take a lie detector test, the prosecutor's office simply didn't feel there was enough evidence to proceed, which certainly wasn't what Carol Schultz had expected. Along with Carol Schultz, though, family members of the North LaSalle Street victims also felt disappointed with the prosecutor's decision not to issue an arrest warrant. They had been in contact with Schultz, who'd convinced them that she had solved the murders of their loved ones. On October 24, 1994, Ted Gierse, Bob Gierse's brother, delivered a scathing letter to Marion County Prosecutor Jeff Modisett. In it, he told Modisett how disappointed he was that the Prosecutor's Office wouldn't be pursuing charges based on the new evidence recovered by Carol Schultz. Ted said that, because of this new evidence, he had changed his belief that the North LaSalle Street murders had been committed for business reasons to now considering jealousy as the motive. He pleaded with the Prosecutor's Office to do something.

Prosecutor Jeff Modisett, on October 25, 1994, answered Ted Gierse's letter, explaining why his office didn't want to proceed with the case. Modisett said that while he would love to solve the most notorious crime in Marion County history, the evidence Carol Schultz had provided was extremely weak, and he believed the witnesses (Chastain and Cavanaugh) were simply caught up in the excitement and attention they were getting because of being involved in the case. Furthermore, he said, the statements of the two witnesses were too contradictory to use in a trial, which they would almost certainly lose. Any good defense attorney would tear their statements apart. (Chastain, for example, had originally said that he had been working at a garage when a man came in covered with blood and told him he had gotten $30,000 to kill the three men. Then Chastain's story changed to himself as the getaway driver.) For these reasons, prosecution simply wasn't possible.

On October 29, 1994, Horton called Ted Gierse long-distance. Horton told him that his health was failing because of the accusations against him, but that he had nothing to do with the killings. He then told Ted that he was a small man, and that it would have taken someone a whole lot bigger than him to control and kill these three guys. He also claimed that he had taken a lie detector test about the murders and passed it (though he actually never took one). Finally, Horton told Gierse's

brother that he believed Ted Uland was the one who had
committed the murders, and that he had phoned Uland
the previous year but found out from his widow that he
had passed away, so he decided to drop it.

The year 1994 passed without any change in the status of the North LaSalle Street case. The prosecutor refused to do anything with just what evidence Carol
Schultz had. Then, in March of 1995, Carol Schultz said
she received some startling new information about the
North LaSalle Street murders; information that could
make the case famous worldwide and her book an instant
bestseller: The Nixon White House might have been
involved.

Schultz said that she received a telephone call from
Floyd Chastain, who said he wanted to tell her about a
secret meeting he'd attended a few nights after the North
LaSalle Street murders. According to Schultz, Chastain
told her that he and Big Mike had driven a semitrailer
to Louisville to drop off a load, then drove over to Bowl-
ing Green, Kentucky, to pick up another load, which they
then brought back to Indianapolis. Chastain, thinking
their job was through, got ready to leave, but Big Mike
told him no, to hang around, they had to go to a meeting.

Big Mike, Chastain claimed, then got on the telephone, and a little later, around 1:00 A.M., a limousine
pulled up. They got into it and were driven to Tommy's
Starlight Palladium Bar, where they attended a meeting

with White House aide Chuck Colson and Jimmy Hoffa (who, Chastain said, must have been on a furlough from prison). Norman Flick, the owner of the bar, also attended the meeting. Chastain said the bar had a number of other people, regular customers, in it that night, though they sat separately from the rest. He didn't really take part in the meeting, he said, but simply sat back and witnessed it. The meeting, Chastain claimed, concerned getting Hoffa a pardon from the president then, Richard Nixon. Chastain told Schultz that at the meeting Colson had Hoffa sign some papers. Then, Chastain's story went, Colson asked if the three men on North LaSalle Street were dead. When someone answered yes, Colson nodded and then said that he needed the microfilm the murderers had apparently been sent to find. According to Chastain, somebody went out and transferred the microfilm to Colson's car. The implication Chastain gave was that the murders on North LaSalle Street had been committed in order to get back some microfilm that had been at the house, microfilm the Nixon White House wanted for some reason, and that Jimmy Hoffa had been the one who'd arranged the murders and retrieval of the microfilm in exchange for a presidential pardon.

Naturally, this story raises a number of questions and stretches credibility considerably. Revelations of a secret meeting between Chuck Colson and Jimmy Hoffa in a bar owned by an organized crime figure would have been as devastating to the White House as Watergate, particularly since the White House eventually granted Jimmy Hoffa executive clemency. In addition, Chastain's story was full of potential witnesses to this supposedly top secret meeting, from the bar populated by regulars to the waitress who he said came by with food and drinks, to his own inexplicable presence at a meeting that had nothing to do with him. This story had all the attributes of a bad spy movie, with the secret White House meeting with an imprisoned Teamsters president at a bar reputed to be owned by an organized crime figure. It was like a conspiracy theory holiday.

In addition to all of this, if a meeting such as this had occurred, it certainly wouldn't have been at Tommy's Starlight Palladium Bar, a lowbrow tavern in a working-class neighborhood, where the limousine Chastain said he and Big Mike drove up in would certainly have attracted attention, not to mention the presence of someone as easily recognizable as Jimmy Hoffa. Truck drivers routinely patronized Tommy's Starlight Palladium Bar and would have known who Hoffa was. Someone would have bragged about seeing him there. There is simply no way it would have stayed a secret.

Yet for unclear reasons, Carol Schultz apparently accepted Chastain's story as the truth, and from that moment on became totally convinced of a White House involvement in the North LaSalle Street murders.

Tying in another previously dismissed theory, Schultz also said that Chastain told her he had been the one who had stripped down the stolen black Corvette that had belonged to murder victim John Terhorst. Following this revelation, Schultz then began suspecting that the White House might have also been involved in the Terhorst murder. In one of the notes she sent to Detective Jon Layton, Schultz said she wondered if Charles Colson had driven a black Corvette.

During 1995, Schultz kept in close contact with Detective Layton. She would send him tapes of her conversations with Horton, White House material she had obtained, and other pieces of information she felt supported her new belief that the North LaSalle Street murders had been committed by the Teamsters in order to win a pardon for Jimmy Hoffa from President Nixon. Along with one of the tapes of her conversations with Horton, Schultz sent a note to Detective Layton saying that she believed this tape had the answers she had been looking for: that Norman Flick, apparently acting as an intermediary for Jimmy Hoffa, had paid Carroll Horton to commit the North LaSalle Street murders. However, on the tape, Horton is actually trying to tell her that he suspected Ted Uland had been the North LaSalle Street murderer.

It's Schultz, however, who dismissed that idea and insisted it was Hoffa, Nixon, the Teamsters, and Norman Flick who were involved. Basically, a review of the tape made by Carol Schultz showed it to be just a conversation with an older man who was trying to sound important and knowledgeable to a pretty young woman, and finally was willing to agree with anything that would make her happy.

Interestingly, Schultz, in her research, managed to

obtain copies of several White House documents relating to the Jimmy Hoffa case. In one dated May 26, 1970, a White House official reported that a man named Harry Singer had contacted him about getting a pardon or parole for Jimmy Hoffa, who had then been in prison for three and a half years. But the official said in the report that he told Singer all such matters were handled by the Justice Department, and that is where he should go with his request.

In another White House document, this one dated March 19, 1971, John W. Dean III, counsel to the president, sent a memorandum to Attorney General John Mitchell. In this memorandum Dean tells Mitchell that Frank Fitzsimmons of the Teamsters Union had called him and requested that he, and Hoffa's wife and son, be allowed to meet with the president in order to talk about Hoffa's parole hearing coming up on March 31. Dean then suggested that such a meeting could work to the advantage of the president and offered several scenarios for the meeting, the gist of Dean's strategy being that President Nixon do as little as possible for Hoffa but leave him feeling that he owed a debt to the White House. The president, Dean said, should be sympathetic and give the vague impression that he felt Hoffa had been the subject of a Kennedy vendetta.

On January 14, 1972, in another document, a White House staffer sent Charles Colson a summary of the news media's reaction to Jimmy Hoffa's December 23, 1971, release from prison. Finally, Schultz also managed to get copies of Charles Colson's White House calendar for December 1971.

All of this made for fascinating reading, particularly for someone who lived during this time. However, nowhere in this material was there any mention of, or connection to, the North LaSalle Street killings. The only thing that tied them together at all was that they all happened in the early 1970s.

Still, as with the accusation that Horton had been the North LaSalle Street killer, Schultz seemingly accepted this new story about a White House connection without question. In fact, Schultz said she wondered if perhaps a connection to the White House was why the local prosecutor wouldn't make an arrest. (Since she personally felt there was more than ample evidence for an arrest, clearly there had to be another reason.) She also said that she tried a number of times to interview Chuck Colson, but that he wouldn't agree to meet with her. She even claimed to have received threats, warning her that she would be killed if she tried to interview Colson.

Schultz also said in her book that one afternoon, during the time she was attempting to get an interview with Colson, a dark-haired man in a plain car pulled into her driveway and then just sat there and watched her house as he talked on his cell phone. She said that he sat there for a long time. Although Schultz said that she sneaked out and wrote down his license plate number, she doesn't explain why she didn't call the police.

While the stories Chastain told Schultz kept getting

more involved and more complex, he soon began to feel uneasy about what he'd told her and the police. And for good reason.

"I told Chastain that he was likely going to be charged with murder in this case, and that it might be a death penalty case," said Detective Charles Briley. "That's when his story started changing and the letters where he said he'd been lying started coming."

Chastain, on March 30, 1993, wrote a letter addressed to McAtee and Popcheff, in which he said that everything he'd told the detectives who had interviewed him was a lie. He said that part of the information he gave to the detectives he had gotten from newspaper articles that Carol Schultz had sent him, and part of it he'd just made up. He said that he lied because he wanted to get even with Horton (apparently over a failed invention that he and Horton had worked on that Chastain thought Horton was getting rich off of). Later, however, Chastain said that the letter he sent to McAtee and Popcheff saying he was lying was a lie, and he only wrote it because he thought that was what the detectives who interviewed him wanted him to do. He said that his original statement was the truth.

On December 25, 1995, Chastain wrote another letter, this one addressed to Christ and Briley, who had interviewed him in Florida. In this letter, he said that he was sorry, but that he had lied to everyone about the North LaSalle Street murders. He said that he made up the part about Jimmy Hoffa and the Teamsters because the detectives had shown him the picture of a man with a Teamsters jacket on, and so he'd incorporated that detail into his story. He also said that the reason he'd lied was because he hoped that the authorities would bring him to Indianapolis, so he could visit with his family. But more importantly, he said, he wanted to finally meet Carol Schultz because they were in love with each other. (The two of them had only had contact over the telephone and through the mail.)

In her response to Floyd Chastain's profession of love, Carol Schultz, according to an article in the May 9, 1996, issue of the *Indianapolis Star*, told Chastain on the telephone that she loved him, too. However, in an article in the August 11, 1996, issue of the *Indianapolis Star*, she insisted that she'd meant she loved him as a Christian. Apparently, however, that wasn't how Chastain had taken it. Chastain told the police he wanted to marry Schultz, and that he had even sent her a ring from prison.

Carol Schultz, while facing opposition from a Prosecutor's Office that wouldn't issue the arrest warrant she wanted, eventually found that some of her former coworkers in the newspaper business were also beginning to question the credibility of her investigation. In the April 11, 1996, issue of the *Indianapolis Star*, a reporter tells of an interview with a man named Carl E. Kierner, who said he knew Carroll Horton, Mary Cavanaugh, and Floyd Chastain. Although at the time of the interview in 1996 Kierner owned a taxicab company, in the 1970s he had worked in Horton's garage. He told the reporter that he couldn't believe it when he heard the news of Horton being accused of the North LaSalle Street murders. Kierner said he was stunned because *he* was the one who had introduced both Chastain and Cavanaugh to Horton, and that the introductions had taken place long after 1971. Kierner told the reporter that in the mid-1970s Floyd Chastain had come into Horton's business looking for parts for a car he was working on. He said that he then introduced Chastain to Carroll Horton, who eventually hired Chastain as a mechanic. Reportedly, Chastain and Horton became very close and worked together attempting to design an engine that could run on alcohol and acetylene. The idea didn't work, and soon afterward Chastain ended up in prison. According to Kierner, though, for some reason Chastain had believed that the idea had actually worked, and that Horton had made a million dollars off of it. Kierner said that Chastain then began calling and threatening Horton, claiming that he had been cheated out of his share of the profits.

Kierner also said that in the 1970s, *he* had been dating Mary Cavanaugh, who he recalled had been a very attractive woman, although a heavy drinker. She apparently had a car that needed a new engine, and so he had it towed to Horton's garage. In January 1974, he told the reporter, he introduced Cavanaugh to Horton. The two of them hit it off right away and developed a very close relationship. Kierner said that Horton helped Cavanaugh financially, and even babysat for her children.

Along with Carl Kierner's list of discrepancies in the story Cavanaugh told, however, Carol Schultz herself said that Chastain had first told her that it had been a woman named Diane (Carroll Horton's ex-wife) who had been in the house on the night of the murders. His story changed later, though, and the woman became Mary Cavanaugh.

Another news story appeared two weeks later that cast even further doubt on the credibility of Carol Schultz's investigation. In an April 28, 1996, article in the *Indianapolis Star*, a reporter tells about interviewing a friend of Carroll Horton's named Joe Chapman, whose mother-in-law, Verna Fisher, had been murdered. Chapman told the reporter that Schultz contacted him and said that she knew who had killed Verna, and that she was interested in the reward they had offered. Schultz had left her job at the *Indianapolis News* several years earlier and perhaps needed the money.

Schultz then met with the family and let them hear an audiotape of a conversation she'd had with Chastain, in which he talked about Fisher's murder. (Apparently, Chastain had confided to Schultz that Horton killed Verna.) Chapman said he had the feeling, though, that Schultz was actually more interested in solving the North LaSalle Street killings than his mother-in-law's. Nevertheless, according to the article, Chapman and his wife accompanied Schultz to her home, where Chapman said he was surprised to see that Schultz apparently had some of the original crime scene photos from the North La-Salle Street case. When Schultz had to leave the house for a few minutes, Chapman said he and his wife looked around and found stacks of love letters addressed to

Schultz from Chastain. The article tells that in one of the letters from Chastain he said that he was sure Schultz could help get him out of prison. They would then be married.

Feeling unsure of Carol Schultz now, the Chapmans said they wanted to test her, so they told her that they were going to lay a trap for Carroll Horton by telling him that Floyd Chastain's sister had some incriminating evidence with his fingerprints on it hidden in her house. However, in fact, they didn't contact Horton at all.

The next day, according to the article, Schultz called the Chapmans and said that their trap had worked perfectly. Schultz told them that Chastain's sister had called her and said that Horton had contacted her and threatened her if she didn't destroy the incriminating evidence. As far as the Chapmans were concerned, Schultz's credibility had been shattered.

Schultz's credibility with law enforcement also began to falter. The police officers involved in the renewed investigation of the North LaSalle Street murders really weren't interested in Schultz's increasingly odd beliefs that the murders had been carried out by Jimmy Hoffa in exchange for executive clemency from President Nixon. In one note Schultz sent to Detective Jon Layton, she told him that Sherriff McAtee didn't want to hear about Hoffa. Eventually, Detective Layton also wouldn't want to hear from Schultz. Before then, however, Schultz told Layton that all she wanted to do was to meet with Chuck Colson and play Chastain's tape about the meeting at

Tommy's Starlight Palladium Bar. She said she wanted to look him in the eye and have him deny it. But Colson continued to refuse to meet with her. Schultz told Detective Layton about an unsuccessful attempt to interview Chuck Colson while he was attending an event in Tennessee, leading her to believe even more in Chastain's story. She believed it even though she herself later said that she knew Chastain had been reading up on Hoffa in books at the prison library.

As for Floyd Chastain, despite changing his story several times, recanting his statements, and then recanting his recantation, he wasn't through yet with his revelations. After telling Schultz about the meeting between White House aide Chuck Colson and Jimmy Hoffa, Chastain later also wrote Schultz a letter in which he claimed he was involved in the murder of Jimmy Hoffa. He even drew her a map of where they had buried Hoffa's body.

Despite the changed stories and recantations, through her conversations with Chastain, Carol Schultz became sold on the idea that the North LaSalle Street murders had been part of a much larger national conspiracy. She became convinced that the victims on North LaSalle Street had somehow gotten their hands on top secret microfilm that could damage the Nixon White House. As a result, she believed, the White House had arranged to have them murdered in order to get the microfilm back. She believed this unreservedly.

Yet still, the Prosecutor's Office refused to issue arrest

warrants, no matter how much she felt they should. But in November 1994, Prosecutor Jeff Modisett lost in the general election and a new prosecutor came into office in January 1995. Schultz was elated and became determined to make this new prosecutor acknowledge the proof she believed she had. She was sure she would get the arrest warrant she wanted, and the case would be closed.

CHAPTER TEN

The new prosecutor, Republican Scott Newman, came into office in Marion County, Indiana, on January 1, 1995, replacing Democrat Jeffrey Modisett. While Modisett had sensed that the case against Carroll Horton was weak at best, and as a result hadn't allowed it to be prosecuted, Newman apparently didn't agree. Carol Schultz claimed that when running for office, Newman had pledged to do everything he could to solve the decades-old triple murder. After being elected, he kept his word and sent the case against Horton to the local grand jury for review, which then looked at it for over a year. The grand jurors heard from a number of witnesses, including Floyd Chastain and Mary Cavanaugh. Carol Schultz, who also testified, said that she had additionally prepared a lengthy written report for them to look at.

On March 6, 1996, the Marion County Prosecutor's

Office held a meeting with Prosecutor Newman, Deputy Prosecutors Sheila Carlisle and Ralph Staples, Wendy Hinson (daughter of victim Robert Hinson), and Ted Gierse. According to notes from the meeting, Newman told the gathering that although he'd sent the case to the grand jury, he didn't expect them to come back with an indictment. Like Modisett, Newman said he felt that the two main witnesses in the case, Floyd Chastain and Mary Cavanaugh, were totally unreliable.

Newman pointed out how Chastain had changed his story repeatedly, recanting his previous story, and then recanting his recantation. And in the end, Chastain had admitted that all he'd really wanted was just to come back to Indiana to visit with his family and to meet Carol Schultz face-to-face.

In addition, according to the meeting notes, Newman said that the Prosecutor's Office also had problems with Mary Cavanaugh's story. For over twenty years she hadn't said anything about North LaSalle Street, yet upon being hypnotized she recalled it all clearly. It seemed highly unlikely. Newman said that as far as he was concerned he didn't think that either Chastain or Cavanaugh had been in the house that night. Their stories, he insisted, simply didn't coincide.

At this meeting, Ted Gierse, naturally disappointed that his brother's murder was apparently going to stay unsolved, asked that Newman and his staff then look at the possibility that Ted Uland had been involved in the triple murder. The prosecutor, however, didn't support this idea, pointing out the futility of it since Uland was dead. Ted Gierse then gave the prosecutor several other names to investigate.

However, just over two weeks later, on March 22, 1996, much to the shock of everyone in the Prosecutor's Office, the Marion County Grand Jury returned an indictment against Carroll Horton for three counts of murder. After looking at the case for over a year, they felt an arrest should be made. Consequently, in a press release the same day, Prosecutor Scott Newman said: "The Grand Jury has spoken and directed us to prosecute, and we will do so to the best of our ability."

This decision by the grand jury should have elated Carol Schultz. She had been trying for years to get this very thing accomplished. However, even though she had been the one to relentlessly pursue these charges against Horton, she felt sorry for him, and close to him, too. They had spoken, she said, almost every day for nearly four years. They had become friends and confidants. She recalled in her book that she cried when she saw the television coverage of him being arrested and taken away in handcuffs.

On March 26, 1996, Carroll Horton had his initial hearing in Criminal Court 1 in downtown Indianapolis. At an initial hearing the judge must decide if there is enough evidence to hold someone for trial. Judge Lapossa, hearing only limited testimony, felt that there was indeed enough evidence for a trial and so ordered Horton to be held in jail without bond.

The grand jury, on March 29, 1996, also returned an indictment against Floyd Chastain, but in his case for only one count of murder, that of Robert Hinson, the victim he told Schultz he had been forced to kill. The news media reported that the indictment was based mostly, though not entirely, on Chastain's own statements.

As might be imagined, the indictments and arrests in this nearly twenty-five-year-old triple murder case caused a considerable media frenzy, both locally and nationally. On the surface it appeared to be an incredible story: A single mother, working mostly alone, had solved a triple murder case that had baffled the police for a quarter century. Schultz said she received requests to appear on *Good Morning America, CBS This Morning,* and *The CBS Evening News* with Dan Rather, while also claiming she tried to stay away from a camera crew filming for *Inside Edition.* In the April 25, 1996, issue of the *Indianapolis Star,* an article told of Carol Schultz's attempts to interest a movie production company, Dream City Films, into producing a movie the article claimed she wanted titled *The Carol Schultz Story.* Also, according to the article, Schultz had persuaded Chastain to sign a power of attorney document that allowed her to handle his end of the movie deal, and had even sent a contract for Carroll Horton to sign for his part in the proposed film.

On May 2, 1996, Carroll Horton, now represented by attorney Richard Kammen, petitioned the court to have a bond set for him. His attorney argued that the evidence against his client was so weak that bond was appropriate. At this hearing, Lieutenant Michael Popcheff and retired lieutenant Jim Strode testified. According to news reports, Strode said that during their original investigation in 1971 Carroll Horton had not been their prime suspect. Rather, he said, their key suspect had been Ted Uland.

On May 3, 1996, during a continuation of the bond hearing, Floyd Chastain admitted to the court that he had been given information about the North LaSalle Street case by several people, including Carol Schultz. And while he had told five different versions about what had supposedly happened that night, he said that he had recanted his recantation, not because it wasn't true, but as reverse psychology, believing that it would make the detectives work harder. According to newspaper accounts, one of the detectives who interviewed Chastain in Florida, Charles Briley, said he had found that a number of the original crime scene photographs were missing. He suspected that Carol Schultz had them and had shown them to Chastain.

In Indiana, usually there is no bond for murder. A murder suspect must remain in jail until trial. Only in cases in which a judge finds that the state's case is extremely weak can a bond for a murder suspect be set. Judge Lapossa apparently felt that this case fit that exception. After hearing testimony from both sides, Judge Lapossa, on May 6, 1996, ordered Horton released on a $5,000 surety bond. According to an article in that day's issue of the *Indianapolis Star*, Judge Lapossa had reportedly even seriously considered releasing Horton on his own recognizance. One of the reasons Judge Lapossa set this very low bail, the newspaper said, was that Detective Jon Layton had apparently found some evidence important to the case in a shed at his home. Layton had earlier testified that this evidence had been turned over to the grand jury. Another reason was that the judge felt that the two main witnesses for the prosecution, Floyd Chastain and Mary Cavanaugh, were not credible at all.

Judge Lapossa was also extremely critical of the credibility of Carol Schultz. She stated, "The court finds that the investigation was compromised by the meddling of Carol Schultz, who is a very biased former investigative reporter."

On the same day, following Judge Lapossa's release of Horton on bail, Marion County Prosecutor Scott Newman called a press conference. At this meeting with the news media, he announced that his office was dropping all charges in the North LaSalle Street case. Newman said that the case had been hurt by Floyd Chastain changing his story over and over, by Carol Schultz being allowed to have access to key police evidence, by the question of the credibility of Mary Cavanaugh, and by the fact that Detective Layton had found the box of evidence in a shed at his house, evidence the grand jury should have seen before making its decision. He felt that all of these circumstances made the case no longer prosecutable. Newman told the media, "There is absolutely no hope of conviction."

After this announcement, Ted Gierse told the news media that he felt very disappointed by the events. He said that he was angry with the police but also felt that he had been duped by Carol Schultz. It had been twenty-five years since his brother's murder, and the police were no closer to solving it than they had been in 1971.

Before the case collapsed, the media frenzy it had caused, including the possibility of a movie deal and all of the national talk shows and news programs requesting interviews with her, had no doubt excited Schultz. It was an incredible amount of attention. However, media interest can sometimes be a double-edged sword. Due to her investigation and the resulting indictments, Schultz had naturally taken part in a number of local news media interviews. One of these interviews with a local television station took place in her home, where the cameraman filmed the notebooks and diaries she had kept of her investigation.

Later, Carol Schultz said that she was both shocked and appalled when a judge ordered her to turn over her notebooks and diaries to the prosecutor so that copies could be made and given to Carroll Horton's defense attorney. This attorney had seen the documents during the Schultz television interview, and afterward petitioned the court to have access to them. The attorney argued that under the rules of discovery (the legal right of a defense attorney to have access to the prosecution's evidence) his client had a right to view the notebooks and diaries.

The court agreed and issued a subpoena for Schultz to produce them. This upset Schultz because she said she felt it to be an invasion of her privacy. Her notebooks, she said, held her most intimate thoughts about Horton and the case, as well as details about very personal parts

of her private life. She felt certain they would be cop-
ied and passed around for everyone to read and enjoy.
Schultz also said later that she felt a part of the reason
that her notebooks and diaries had been subpoenaed and
taken away was because certain officials were jealous of
her fame. According to Schultz, she, not the police, had
solved the twenty-five-year-old murders; they were trying to get even with her.

Schultz said in the book she wrote about her investigation that when she brought the notebooks and diaries
to the Prosecutor's Office, she sensed hostility among
the staff. She said that when she handed over the materials, a female prosecutor ordered an aide to make a copy
of every single page. Schultz also recalled that on the
same day she turned in her notebooks and diaries, she
had to attend a meeting with two deputy prosecutors and
Horton's defense attorney. Schultz claimed that as the
defense attorney questioned her about her relationship
with Horton, the prosecutors became alarmed by the
questions and her answers, and cut the meeting short.
The prosecutors said that they'd have to reschedule it for
another day.

After Horton's defense attorney left, Schultz said that
the two deputy prosecutors came back and had a closed-
door meeting with her, during which they began yelling at her about her appearances on various news media
programs. They said that every time they turned on the
news there she was, and they ordered her not to talk to
any more reporters or to the police. They then asked her
about the information concerning the North LaSalle

Street murders she had sent to Chastain (which would, of course, taint any information he gave to the police). Schultz said she admitted to sending him a newspaper article about the murders.

Also, at least according to Schultz, the meeting got uglier when one of the prosecutors grabbed and started searching her purse, reportedly looking for any information she had about the North LaSalle Street case besides the notebooks and diaries. Then, Schultz said, they accused her of sleeping with the various police officers involved in the case in order to get information from them. Following this, according to Schultz, they began screaming at her about the book she was writing and the reported movie offers. Schultz said she left the meeting in tears.

Once the charges against him had been dropped, Carroll Horton filed a lawsuit against the city of Indianapolis for false arrest, seeking $300,000. Although he presumably had a good case, on January 1, 1999, Horton died before it could come to court. Carol Schultz, when she heard the news about Horton's death, said she was overcome with grief. She couldn't believe it. While Horton had reportedly died of natural causes, Schultz said she couldn't help but wonder if perhaps he had been murdered because of what he knew about the North LaSalle Street killings. Or, Schultz theorized in 2005, maybe Horton had even faked his own death and was still around.

Along with Schultz, Floyd Chastain also continued with his belief in conspiracy theories. He wrote a letter to the *Indianapolis Star* on April 3, 1997, in which he claimed he had proof that the North LaSalle Street murders were linked to the murder of Jimmy Hoffa and to the Nixon White House. Chastain said he was writing the letter because he wanted to have a meeting with prosecutors so that he could give them the information he had. Not surprisingly, the Prosecutor's Office didn't give much credibility to this claim.

To the end, Carol Schultz held on to the belief of Carroll Horton's guilt. In 2005, she said that a source she had inside the Indianapolis Police Department told her that the Homicide Branch had actually received a confession from Carroll Horton, and that because of the confession the case had since been designated as cleared and closed.

Carol Schultz's information was not entirely wrong. The Indianapolis Police Department did eventually receive a confession about the North LaSalle Street murders.

But it wasn't from Carroll Horton.

PART THREE
2000

CHAPTER ELEVEN

On September 11, 2001, the United States suffered the most deadly terrorist attack in its history when two jet airliners, piloted by Al Qaeda operatives, smashed into the twin towers of the World Trade Center in New York City. The impacts not only killed all of the people on the airplanes, but the resulting fireballs also instantly incinerated hundreds of people in the building. Thousands of New York City emergency workers, when they heard of the attack, dropped what they were doing and with no thought for their own safety, raced to the scene. Of the almost 3,000 people who died in these attacks, 403 were emergency workers trapped inside when the towers, weakened by the collision and resulting intense fire, eventually began collapsing. The New York City Police and Fire Departments had never in their history suffered tragedies of this magnitude.

When Detective Sergeant Roy West of the Indianapolis Police Department's Homicide Branch heard about the terrorist attack in New York City, he, like most people, felt shaken and sad. It was a tragedy of a magnitude never experienced before on American soil. However, West, a police officer with almost thirty years of experience, and a veteran of both the Marine Corps and the Air Force Reserve, didn't feel that just giving blood or donating money was enough. He felt he had to do more. He knew it would be a tremendous undertaking in New York City to clear the wreckage and attempt to recover the bodies, which would be in such a shape that identification of them would take a massive effort. The local authorities would need lots of people trained in this area, probably more than they had in New York City.

"I couldn't just sit here in Indianapolis when it was obvious these people needed help," West said. He knew that with his years of work as a homicide detective he could be of assistance in New York City. And so, he asked that he be allowed to take all of his remaining leave time for 2001, a little over five weeks. Upon receiving approval of his leave request, West then called the New York City Police Department, told them of his background as a homicide investigator, and said that he wanted to help in the World Trade Center recovery process. He was told that New York City would be glad to have the assistance of someone with his expertise. They had plenty of work for him to do.

Without worrying about booking a room, West left

Indianapolis for New York City on September 22. The next day, he appeared at the New York City Police Department's Command Center, and soon found himself working at Ground Zero. The cleanup and recovery process was a huge undertaking at Ground Zero, but West's talents would soon be needed elsewhere.

"After a couple of days one of the guys at the Command Center asked me if I had a strong stomach," West recalls. "When I told him I'd been working homicides for fifteen years, he said, 'Good, because we need some help at the morgue.'"

For the next five weeks West worked twelve hours a day at the New York City Morgue, where he assisted the personnel there in identifying the bodies recovered from the wreckage of the World Trade Center, but more often identifying just body parts. The initial explosion of the two aircraft hitting the buildings and the eventual collapse of the two towers had naturally mangled most of the bodies. Some of the victims were so incinerated and mutilated that chances were they would never be identified. But the recovery team had to try. Fortunately, his years of working in homicide had steeled Roy West for this gruesome task.

When West left Indianapolis for New York City, he had made no arrangements for living quarters, figuring he'd find something when he got there. West, however, found that the New York City Police Department took very good care of him. "They at first put me up in a hotel," West said. "But the authorities had been asking

New Yorkers to open their homes to us, and so for most of the time I was there I stayed with some really nice people. The people there were just wonderful."

By the time West had to return to his job in Indianapolis, he found that in the short time he had been in New York City he'd made many friends and had earned the gratitude of everyone he met during the World Trade Center recovery process. The enormity of the tragedy and the dedication of the people involved in the recovery process became a strong bonding mechanism for those involved.

"I've never become so close to a group of people in such a short time as I did in New York," West said.

He recalled how, whenever the recovery teams would bring the body of a slain emergency worker to the morgue, the police would line both sides of the street and salute as the body passed. It was their way of recognizing the devotion to duty the person had shown. On the night he left to go back to Indianapolis, someone contacted his driver and told him to return to the morgue because West had forgotten something. When the car pulled up to the morgue West saw that police officers had lined up on both sides of the street and were saluting him as he passed. He said he had never in his life received as great an honor.

When Detective West finally returned to Indianapolis, news of his sacrifice and service in New York City circulated around the police department. Soon, his story also reached the ears of several members of the local news media, who recognized a great human-interest story and contacted West, asking for an interview. To their surprise, however, they found that West refused to talk to them about the five weeks he had spent in New York City.

While the news media could understand West's motives for wanting to go to New York City to offer his help, they couldn't fathom his reluctance to talk about it, particularly since he had been on television and in the newspaper dozens of times before as a homicide detective. They simply couldn't understand why someone wouldn't want to receive recognition for extraordinary services. But anyone who knew Roy West wasn't surprised at all.

Roy Steven Francis West joined the Indianapolis Police Department in 1972, and after graduation from the Police Academy served for several years as a uniformed street officer, and then with the Motorcycle Division. In 1983, West asked for and received an assignment to the Narcotics Branch as an undercover officer, and then in 1986, two years after being promoted to sergeant, he transferred to the Homicide Branch to become a homicide unit supervisor. In this assignment, which he held until his retirement at the end of 2007, West directed the activities of four homicide detectives, while also investigating murder cases himself. Even after his retirement from the Indianapolis Police Department, West still continued as an investigator, working for the Marion County Grand Jury.

At first glance, West appeared a very average and

ordinary person: average height, average build, average looks. But as a homicide detective, West stood out as anything but average and ordinary.

Along with the drive to give of himself to those in need and his tremendous modesty (both of which he demonstrated during the World Trade Center recovery process in New York City), West also possessed a number of other personality traits that, while perhaps not as endearing, served him well as a homicide investigator. He never settled for simply doing his job, or even just doing his job well—he routinely took every task he was given over the cliff edge and into the abyss of "doing it to death." The files of his murder investigations were so detailed that they routinely filled up several storage boxes, and he regularly turned in three-page, single-spaced reports on suicide cases (which were typically given only a paragraph or two).

West was so meticulous that his desk and surrounding area became strictly off-limits to everyone in the office. This came about because everything in his work area sat in a specifically designated spot. Nothing was ever scattered about or out of order. At a crime scene, West would not allow anyone, not even his superiors, to cross the crime scene tape until after he had finished searching the area over and over, often driving the crime lab technicians to near madness with the amount of evidence he wanted them to process and collect.

While some of West's personality traits have likely driven his wife and three children to distraction, they also made Roy West arguably the best homicide detective the Indianapolis Police Department had ever seen. There were never questions left unanswered in his cases, no evidence uncollected, no suspects or witnesses not interrogated. West never abandoned cases because they looked unsolvable. Because of his work habits, most of the prosecutor's staff loved working with West. They loved it because they knew that with West, they would get a case as thoroughly investigated as humanly possible, with absolutely no detail left out or any task uncompleted. They wouldn't have to, as they did with many other detectives, draw up a list of further items that needed to be investigated or further people who needed to be talked to. It was already done.

Detective Roy West not only solved the ordinary murder cases that came across his desk every year, but also managed to solve the kind of murder cases that other detectives would have labeled unsolvable; cases other detectives would have shelved. One notable instance was his investigation into the murder of sixteen-year-old Shanna Sheese, a case that demonstrated West's persistence, determination, and extraordinary ability to close a case other detectives would have given up on.

On October 19, 1998, a homeless man scavenging for aluminum cans stumbled onto the nude body of a woman hidden in the high weeds of a vacant lot in the 900 block of East Market Street in Indianapolis, just a few blocks from the downtown area. The body, in such a state of decomposition that the cause of death wasn't immediately obvious, appeared to have been dumped there, as the uniformed officers responding to the call couldn't find any of the woman's clothing other than a single sock.

At the Indianapolis Police Department, homicide detectives caught assignments on a rotating basis. Once a detective received a murder investigation, he or she wouldn't receive another one until all of the other detectives on the shift had each received one. Sergeants were the exception. Since they were also responsible for supervising the shift, they received a case assignment on every second rotation. As it turned out, Detective Sergeant Roy West received the case assignment for this murder.

Very little evidence was found at the scene on East Market Street, adding to the belief that the victim had been murdered elsewhere and simply dumped there. The search was no easy task because the area where the body had been dumped had knee-high weeds everywhere. Yet still, West meticulously searched every inch, unfortunately with no success.

Fingerprints taken by the coroner identified the body as that of sixteen-year-old Shanna Sheese. As a part of a murder investigation, the assigned detective will usually attend the autopsy, which most often takes place the next day. The assigned detective needs to be there in order to see the wounds and to see exactly what caused the death. This can become extremely important in a murder case because it can often help narrow the investigation by telling the detective what kind of murder weapon to look for, or even what sort of suspects to pursue (if the manner of death could have been caused only by a certain type of person, such as someone very tall or someone with a lot of strength). When West attended the autopsy of Sheese, he found that she had died from blunt force trauma to the head. No helpful information about the weapon or her attacker was forthcoming, though; it was unknown what had been used to strike her, and anyone could have done it. The autopsy didn't give West much to work with.

For the next few weeks, West canvassed the neighborhood where Sheese's body had been found, looking for clues and talking to dozens of people about the victim. West also talked to Shanna Sheese's family. He learned from Sheese's mother that Shanna had recently given birth (her baby was a month old) and that she had left home on October 12, 1998, the day her father died, apparently distraught over his death. That was a week before her body was found, and they hadn't heard from her again after that.

Sheese's sister showed Detective West some of the locations Shanna had been known to frequent. West visited these areas over and over, handing out fliers about Sheese and hoping to find someone who could give him any information about her or about who would want to kill her. Sometimes the picture of a victim can jog people's memories of an event they had forgotten. Additionally, West put out media alerts for a car that had been seen in the area where Sheese had been found, and even had aerial photographs taken of the area. (Aerial photographs will often show information not always visible from the ground; for example, dropped evidence or access routes to the crime scene, such as a footpath that leads through adjoining property.)

Despite these efforts, West could come up with very little evidence and only very scant information about Sheese. He did, however, uncover the fact that the victim had apparently been a crack addict and had engaged in prostitution in order to pay for her drug habit. This was why the sixteen-year-old's fingerprints had been on file. West also discovered that Sheese had performed most of her prostitution out of a run-down house at 1529 East Michigan Street, on Indianapolis's near east side, less than a mile from where the homeless man had found her body. This brought up the possibility that one of her customers had killed her. However, the only individuals West found in that area who could give him any information about Sheese were the homeless people, drug addicts, and prostitutes who frequented the vicinity, and none of the information they provided proved helpful in his investigation of Sheese's murder.

One day West received information about a large amount of dried blood on Arsenal Avenue, a few blocks from where the homeless man had found Sheese's body. West dropped what he was doing, hurried to the scene, and located this blood, but then tracked it back to an injured animal. West shook his head. Another dead end. It seemed that nothing would come together on this case. Everyplace he turned he came up empty.

"Even though I really worked hard on the Sheese

case," West said, "I couldn't come up with anything substantial at all. I kept drawing a blank."

West's lieutenant, after seeing weeks of fruitless work, finally decided to deactivate the Sheese murder case. This meant that, even though the case was still unsolved, no more active work would be done on it. Homicide branches have to do this with some murder cases, particularly those without substantial leads, in order for their detectives to give more time and attention to new cases, or to cases that do have substantial leads. Of course, if new leads do come up in the deactivated case, it can always be reopened. Often in murder investigations detectives will uncover leads to other murders. Sometimes the same person committed both murders, and sometimes individuals will tell about other murders as part of a plea deal. But until something like this occurs, a deactivated case stays on the shelf. West, however, as was typical with him, couldn't quite make himself give up just yet on the Sheese case.

Although assigned new murder cases to work on, West continued to work the Sheese case whenever he could. Whenever he was close by on another case he would stop in the areas he had earlier canvassed and check for new information or for witnesses he had missed. He also contacted the uniformed officers and the vice and narcotics detectives who worked around 1500 East Michigan Street, letting them know that he was interested in any information they came across concerning Sheese or her murder. While it would seem logical to contact the vice and narcotics detectives (since Sheese had been a known crack addict and a prostitute), West, because of his thoroughness, knew that the uniformed officers could also be great sources of information. They patrol the same areas every day and know most of the people like Sheese who cause them problems. West always believed in tapping every source of information possible.

West also talked several times to his superiors about reopening the case so that he could give it more attention. However, since West had no leads or suspects, he was uniformly told that the case was a dead end and that he needed to let go and move on.

But West's persistence paid off. On January 22, 1999, three months after Shanna Sheese was found and after West had made several follow-up contacts to be certain that both the uniformed officers and the vice and narcotics detectives knew he was still interested in information about Sheese, narcotics detectives brought to Detective West a man who had told them that he had information about the Sheese murder. Individuals regularly involved in criminal activity will hang on to and then use information such as this as currency to buy their way out of jail. There was an expression at the Homicide Branch, "We'll always trade a weenie for a ham," meaning they were always open to dropping or reducing charges on lesser crimes for information on more serious crimes. That was what this man was looking to do.

Ray Harber,[1] a crack addict, told West that he had

---

[1] Denotes pseudonym

recently been at a crack house where he overheard two brothers talking about a murder. Harber said that during the conversation he heard them claim that they had beaten a woman to death with a brick and then left her on a vacant lot, stripping off all of her clothing so that it would look like a john/prostitute murder. The brothers, Harber told West, were named Malcolm and Darrell Wilson. West immediately remembered Malcolm, whom he had talked to right after the Sheese murder. Malcolm had admitted to West that he knew Sheese, but also claimed that he hadn't seen her on the day she died, nor had any information about her murder.

Harber's information, of course, wasn't enough for West to make an arrest, but it did finally give him a suspect and a direction for the investigation. He now became more committed than ever to solving this case.

A month later, on February 22, 1999, after West had also been in touch with the uniformed personnel at the jail and told them that he was interested in any information about Shanna Sheese, Teresa Sessile,[2] who had been incarcerated in the Marion County Jail, contacted him. She told West that while in jail she had talked with a woman named Vanessa Thompson. Thompson, according to Sessile, had bragged that she and Malcolm Wilson had killed Sheese by repeatedly hitting her in the head with a brick.

Then on February 26, 1999, another inmate at the

[2] Denotes pseudonym

Marion County Jail, Beverly Hudson,[3] contacted West. She also had information. Hudson told him that a cellmate of hers, Alexa J. Whedon, had confided to her that on the day of the Sheese murder she had been at a party with Vanessa Thompson, Malcolm Wilson, and Shanna Sheese. According to Whedon, Thompson had previously been Wilson's lover, but he had recently dumped her in favor of Sheese, which had infuriated Thompson. Apparently, Whedon said, Thompson, already angry at Sheese over some drugs she had supposedly stolen, became so incensed when she saw Wilson and Sheese together that she suddenly smashed Sheese in the head with a brick.

Alexa Whedon additionally confided to Hudson that, although in the past she, too, had been involved with Malcolm Wilson, at the time of the murder she was actually in a lesbian relationship with Vanessa Thompson. Because of this, Whedon said, she joined in and also struck Sheese with a brick. She told Hudson that after she and Thompson thought they had killed Sheese, Wilson took her bloodied body to the vacant lot, but as he was getting ready to dump her he found that Sheese was still alive and gasping. So Malcolm Wilson bashed her several more times in the head with a brick and killed her.

Even with all this new information, Detective West knew that it still wouldn't be enough for the staff of the

---

[3] Denotes pseudonym

Prosecutor's Office, since it involved only overheard conversations and unsubstantiated claims. He didn't have enough yet.

"All I had," West said, "was a lot of 'he said, she said.' I knew I needed some hard evidence."

Now that he felt he knew what had actually happened, West began collecting more statements and searching for more evidence. In any free time he had between his other cases, he would visit the murder site and interrogate everyone he could find who might have any knowledge at all about the case. And as will often happen when a person refuses to give up, West's persistence paid off and he soon began accumulating small bits of evidence. Finally, when West felt that he had collected enough evidence, he brought everything he had, including many additional statements he had taken, to the Prosecutor's Office, which then filed murder charges against Wilson, Thompson, and Whedon. In three separate trials, juries found all of the defendants guilty of the murder of Shanna Sheese. Malcolm Wilson received sixty-five years in prison, while Vanessa Thompson and Alexa J. Whedon each received fifty-five years.

This one case, however, was by no means the only time that Detective Roy West demonstrated exceptional ability as a homicide detective. Another investigation that showcased his extraordinary intuitive abilities was West's investigation into the murder of eleven-year-old Lashonna Bates.

On April 5, 1994, a man who said he was searching for a runaway dog in a large wooded area on the northeast side of Indianapolis stumbled onto the extremely decomposed body of Lashonna Bates, who had been reported missing a month and a half earlier from her home over five miles away. According to police reports, Bates had last been seen waiting for a school bus on February 15, 1994. During the autopsy, the pathologist found that Bates had died from blunt force trauma to the head. Although the body was badly decomposed, and later there would be conflicting testimony, the pathologist stated that he didn't believe Bates had been sexually molested.

Steven Guthier, the homicide detective initially assigned to the investigation, worked intensely on the case, interviewing dozens of people and repeatedly canvassing the areas where Bates lived and where she had been found. After hundreds of hours of investigative work, and the assistance of several other homicide detectives, Guthier wasn't able to turn up much evidence or information about what had happened to the little girl. The chief suspect in the case was a relative of Bates, one who had allegedly been sexually molesting her. In fact, Bates's mother had reportedly been planning to turn the relative in to the police on the same day her daughter disappeared. However, the relative had a solid alibi for the time Bates disappeared, and consequently, the case stalled. Eventually, when no arrest was made, Guthier's lieutenant took a look at the investigation, and after reviewing the case status, decided to deactivate it.

Five years later, in 1999, the cold case squad reopened the Bates murder investigation. The cold case squad is a team of homicide detectives who look into old deactivated murder cases in the hope of perhaps finding new witnesses or maybe clues and evidence overlooked in the original investigation. Sometimes, along with trying to find new witnesses and evidence, this unit can also try using new technology that was not available when the original detective investigated the case. In the Bates investigation, however, the cold case squad was unable to find any new evidence or witnesses. They, too, saw the relative as the key suspect and unsuccessfully tried to break down his alibi. After two years of fruitless investigation, the cold case squad was about to deactivate the Bates murder case once more.

Before they could, however, Major Richard Crenshaw, the commander of the Crimes against Persons Bureau, asked that a detective who hadn't been involved in the original case or in the cold case investigation take a fresh look at the file just to be absolutely certain nothing had been missed. Since this crime had involved such a young and totally innocent victim, he didn't want to let it be shelved again if there was any chance at all of solving it. Roy West was the detective assigned this responsibility.

West's uncanny ability as an investigator soon demonstrated itself again. All of the other detectives who had looked into the case, both originally and during the cold case investigation, had focused on the relative who had been molesting Lashonna Bates. West, however, apparently saw something in the file that the other detectives didn't that made him suspect the man who had found the girl's body.

"I saw some things in his statement that struck me as odd," West explained. "Whenever he talked about Lashonna [Bates], he personalized it too much."

West contacted the man and explained to him that he was taking one last look at the case. He didn't want to alarm the man or frighten him into running, so he acted as though everything he was doing was just routine. He asked the man if he would mind coming down to the Homicide Office and answering just a few questions. In addition to being an exceptional detective, West was naturally also a skilled interrogator, and he eventually got the man to confess to the crime and reveal information that had never been released to the news media and would only be known by the murderer.

And so, when in late 2000, a person came forward claiming to have knowledge about who had committed the triple murder on North LaSalle Street, Detective Sergeant Roy West, because of the abilities he had shown in dozens of murder cases, and particularly because of his ability to see things unapparent to other detectives, became the obvious choice to investigate it. With his usual enthusiasm and vigor, West went right to work.

CHAPTER TWELVE

On November 17, 2000, the Indianapolis Police Department Homicide Branch received a telephone call from Deputy Deborah Borchelt of the Gibson County Sheriff's Office. She called to pass along the news that a young woman named Angel Palma had come into her office and said that she had some very important information about a triple murder that had taken place up in Indianapolis. The young woman, however, only had scant information about the murders. Palma told Borchelt that she thought the murders may have occurred in 1971 and that three men had had their throats cut. She went on to tell the deputy that she suspected the killer might have been her father, Fred Robert Harbison, and that he had been hired by another man to kill the three victims.

Police officers often hear stories like this, about someone suspecting someone else of a crime. Usually, the information comes from hearsay or an overheard conversation. Seldom is it based on fact. And so, when Borchelt asked Palma how she knew all of this, expecting to hear a typical story about how someone had told someone else who had told her, Palma instead said that her father had left a letter confessing to the crime in his safety deposit box, only meant to be opened after he died (which he had in 1998). In the letter he told about his involvement in the murders. Now Deputy Borchelt was interested. Deathbed confessions of this sort often contain information about actual crimes.

Consequently, Deputy Borchelt excused herself, told Palma that she would be right back, and then went and contacted the state police post in Indianapolis, where she talked with a Trooper Brooks. In smaller rural counties, such as Gibson, the Sheriff's Office is much more used to dealing with the state police involving murder investigations than with the local police. She told Brooks what Palma had said and asked if there had been such a case in Indianapolis in 1971. Gibson County is about 145 miles southwest of Indianapolis. The news in this area comes more from Evansville (Indiana) and Louisville than from Indianapolis. After a bit of thought, Brooks said he believed Palma must be talking about the North LaSalle Street killings, but that he wasn't positive the date was 1971. He thought it might be later. At any rate, the trooper told Borchelt, it wasn't the state police who had investigated that case. It hadn't fallen within their jurisdiction. The case had been investigated by the Indianapolis Police Department. He gave Borchelt the telephone number of the Indianapolis Police Department Homicide Branch. Borchelt thanked him and then hung up and called the Indianapolis Police Department.

As luck would have it, Deputy Borchelt talked to Sergeant Roy West when she called into the Homicide Office. West listened to her story and then asked the deputy to get a recorded statement from Angel Palma. After she sent him the tape, West told her, he would listen to the interview and, if it seemed like the statement had any veracity to it, an investigator, depending on who got the case, would come down and speak with Palma.

West was well aware of the North LaSalle Street murders. Although they had occurred in the year before he joined the police department, everyone who had lived in Indianapolis during that time knew about them. They had filled the newspapers and television news broadcasts for weeks. But in addition to this, West also had a much closer connection to the case—when it was resurrected in the early 1990s by Carol Schultz, West had been detailed to assist Detective Jon Layton. Although only peripherally involved in the case at that time, doing mostly "gofer" work, West was nevertheless well aware of the major aspects of the case.

When, at West's request, Borchelt went back to speak with Palma, she found the young woman to be very reticent. Palma didn't want to go into much detail about the letter, and seemed particularly nervous about giving a recorded statement. Palma said that right then all she really wanted was just to be certain that a crime such as this had really occurred. Palma said she wasn't 100 percent sure that the information in the letter was true, but she felt she had to check it out.

"Initially she [Palma] was scared," West said. "When she originally brought this information to the Gibson County Sheriff's Office, she was fearful of giving them too much information."

After confirmation from Deputy Deborah Borchelt that such a case had occurred, Angel Palma finally began talking. She said that, according to the letter, her father had been hired to kill the three men so that another man could collect on an insurance policy. When asked by Deputy Borchelt, Palma refused to give the name of the man who had hired her father but said that she would possibly give it later if the information in the letter proved accurate. At this time, Palma said she wasn't totally certain that the letter wasn't just a hoax or joke. She wanted to be absolutely sure that the facts in the letter were true before she gave out too much information. Also, she believed that the man her father claimed had commissioned the killings still lived in nearby Jasper, Indiana, and so Palma said that she was worried about the safety of herself and her two children if she accused him of murder.

In the letter, Palma continued, her father stated that the reason he was writing it was because he had been cheated out of the money he had been promised for the killings. He said in the letter that he had warned the man who hired him that he was going to write the letter and put it in his lockbox at the bank. If he wasn't paid by the time he died, his wife would send the letter to the police.

This was all the information that Palma wanted to

give at the time. However, she left promising to come back in and bring the letter.

"Naturally, I was skeptical about the letter in the beginning," said West, "given the amount of time that had passed and the publicity the case had gotten." West had not forgotten the huge amount of publicity—not just local, but also national—that Carol Schultz had generated with the case.

Three days later, Angel Palma again showed up at the Gibson County Sheriff's Office, this time upset and disheveled. She told the deputies that earlier that day she had been involved in a disturbance with her uncle, Jeff Pankake, and that two officers who had been called to the scene had taken her to the local hospital in handcuffs, but that the hospital had later released her. Palma said that she had intended to come to the Sheriff's Office that day and bring them the letter from her father, but that it had disappeared from her purse during all of the ruckus surrounding her being handcuffed and taken to the hospital. It had been in her purse, she said, when she arrived at her uncle's house, but then it wasn't there when the police gave her the purse back later. She didn't know what had happened to it.

Deputy Borchelt, after listening to Palma's story, contacted the police department in Princeton, Indiana, where the disturbance with Palma had occurred. The officers involved in the incident said that when they arrived at the scene they had spoken with Jeff Pankake. He showed the officers where Palma, during the disturbance, had apparently broken several windows in his car.

She had been so upset that Pankake asked the two offi-cers to take her to the local hospital for observation. Pan-kake would later tell West that Palma was having a very difficult time dealing emotionally with the revelations about her father, a man she had adored, and that she ap-parently took her frustration out on his car windows.

When the officers who had responded to the distur-bance call spoke with Palma, she told them about the letter she was bringing to the Sheriff's Office. She told the officers that she had come over and shown the letter to her uncle. The officers said that they then went and asked Pankake about the letter, and he showed them a scanned copy of it on his computer. Pankake, appar-ently having realized that in Palma's emotional condition anything could happen to the letter, had scanned it as a precaution. After scanning it, Pankake said he gave the original back to Angel Palma. Palma apparently still had the original in her purse, but in her excited condi-tion the officers likely wanted to speak with someone calmer, so they went to Jeff Pankake. The officers verified to Borchelt that the letter had talked about some mur-ders in Indianapolis, where the victims had had their throats cut.

While at the Sheriff's Office, Palma spoke further about the letter from her father's safety deposit box. She said that when she had shown the letter to her uncle, Jeff Pankake, he, like her, had been shocked by the contents. Palma had apparently been so upset when she arrived at her uncle's house that Pankake at first didn't believe her when she told him about the letter. She had to show it to him to make him believe her. She was apparently hoping that Pankake would tell her that it wasn't true; it was just a hoax. But he didn't.

"Pankake at first had some reservations about Palma and thought she was making the story up," said West. "Until he saw the letter."

Palma told Deputy Borchelt that after Pankake had scanned the letter into his computer, she didn't know what happened to it. She swore she had put it back into her purse, along with a photocopy of the letter she had found in the same area where she had found the original. They were both gone when she got her purse back after the hospital released her. She told Deputy Borchelt that she had finally decided that she wanted the police to know everything about the letter because if it was true, then the families of the victims deserved to know what had happened to their loved ones. Borchelt tried to question Palma again about the man who had hired her father, but Palma said she couldn't talk about it right then. She was too upset. The deputy suspected that Palma still feared what the man might do if he found out that she had informed on him. Palma promised she would come into the Sheriff's Office the next day.

The following day, Angel Palma did show up at the Gibson County Sheriff's Office and once more talked with Deputy Deborah Borchelt. Palma had apparently gotten over her fear of naming the man who had hired her father, because she had just found out that he had died a number of years before. She went on to tell Deputy Borchelt that in the letter her father said that he had been hired to do the killing by a man named Ted Uland. Her father, she said, had worked for Uland's oil drilling company, performing various jobs around the oil wells.

She told Borchelt that her father hadn't gone far in school and didn't speak grammatically correct English. The letter, she said, was worded just as her father would have spoken. In it, Palma said, her father had stated that he was only supposed to kill two men, but then had been forced to kill a third because he had shown up unexpectedly. Her father also talked in the letter about how the police said that there had been a yellow Oldsmobile seen at the murder site, but that it had actually been his yellow Plymouth Road Runner. Her father went on to tell how he buried the boots he had worn that night because he knew that he had left tracks in the blood and that the police could match them to him.

Palma told Deputy Borchelt that the original letter had been in a sealed envelope addressed to the "Chief of Police, Police Dept., Indianapolis, Ind." She also said that a photocopy of the letter had been in another envelope addressed to the *Indianapolis Star* newspaper.

She had found the letters, Palma told Deputy Borchelt, when she was going through her father's stuff, reminiscing. She and her father had been extremely close, and she was looking for photos or other remembrances of him. Both letters had sat for years in a safety deposit box, but after her father died, her stepmother had emptied the box and taken the contents home, apparently without going through them. Palma said she found one of the letters stuffed into a larger envelope containing an insurance policy and a few other items of her father's personal belongings. She added that, after reading it, at first she didn't believe it could be true. She thought it must be some kind of hoax. This wasn't the father she knew. It had to be some kind of joke.

Palma said that she and her uncle had searched the computer for any information about a triple murder in Indianapolis in 1971 in which three men had had their throats cut but couldn't find anything. (In 2000, Google was still only a small company, and computer search engines did not have the power they do today. And Pankake and Palma didn't have any names, exact dates, or addresses to go on, either.) But still, Palma said, she felt she had to be certain, and that was why she came to the Sheriff's Office. She added that the letters had been sealed when she found them and that her stepmother didn't know about their contents. Her stepmother told her that her father had talked about the letters—not what was in them but what to do with them—a number of times over the years, but that after he died she had forgotten about them.

During the interview, Palma also added that her biological mother had once told her a story that she had never believed was true about another murder that her father had supposedly committed. She said her mother told her that her father had been hired to kill a man, and that he was supposed to make the killing look like a revenge murder for messing around with another man's wife. Her father, according to Palma's mother, had killed the man and then cut off his penis. Palma finished by telling the deputy that when she was growing up, her father had had a reputation as being a man who would kill you if you messed with him. But she said she'd never really believed it. To her, he was always a kind, loving man.

When, on November 21, 2000, Sergeant Roy West received all of this information from the Gibson County Sheriff's Office, he immediately asked to be assigned to the case, and wanted authorization to travel to southern Indiana to look into this supposed letter.

Naturally, his superiors were suspicious of this information. The North LaSalle Street murders had been the most widely publicized murders in Indianapolis history, and the police had received many false leads over the years (including, most recently, Carroll Horton). There had been many men who, to either impress or scare, had told someone that they had committed the North LaSalle Street murders. A little checking would usually prove these to be empty boasts.

But also of concern in reopening this case was that, along with it being the most notorious case in the history of the Indianapolis Police Department, it had also been one of the most embarrassing. In 1971, the police department had made a number of public announcements about how the case would be solved soon, about how the police were closing in on the perpetrators and arrests were imminent. Of course, none of that happened, and as the police department became more and more anxious for a solid lead, stories such as how they'd even gone so far as to bring in a psychic in the hope that he could help solve the case all added to the embarrassment.

But while this was bad enough, there was the more recent fiasco in the mid 1990s with Carol Schultz, who'd succeeded in resurrecting the case with considerable fanfare until, much to the embarrassment of the police department, it fell to pieces. In the end, the chief of police had disciplined several of the officers involved in the handling of the reopened case.

So naturally, the police department administration was very skeptical and nervous about any new investigation into a case that had already blown up in their face twice. Yet still, it was obvious that information like this could not just be ignored without looking into it, so Sergeant West got his assignment, and the approval to travel to southern Indiana. Most importantly, he needed to obtain the original copy of the letter, if at all possible. That would be the key to making the case.

Before West traveled to southern Indiana, though, on November 23, 2000, Thanksgiving Day, he was working in the Homicide Office. The day before, Pankake had faxed him a copy of the letter written by Fred Harbison, the one he had scanned into his computer, and West was going over it for the tenth time.

On the copy of the letter faxed to him, West had found that the writer, Fred Harbison, said that he had been hired by Ted Uland to kill two men up in Indianapolis so that Uland could collect on insurance policies he had on them. Harbison stated that he had killed two of the men in their beds by slitting their throats, and that "there was a nother [*sic*] guy there who was not suppose [*sic*] to be but I had to kill him to [*sic*] because he was there." Harbison claimed in the letter that Uland was supposed to pay him for the murders when the insurance paid off, but that Uland never did because he claimed he lost the money.

Confirming what Angel Palma had earlier told the police, Harbison went on to write that when he wasn't paid he warned Uland that he would put a letter in his lockbox at the bank telling all about the murders, and that if he died before being paid, the letters would be sent by his wife to the police and the newspaper. (He also stated that his wife didn't know anything about the murders. He had told her, he wrote, that Uland owed him a large poker debt.) Harbison also mentioned in the letter that the yellow car seen at the murder site had been his yellow Road Runner, and that he had buried the boots he'd worn because he knew he had stepped in blood and left tracks.

After reading the letter again and again, West called Pankake on the telephone.

Jeff Pankake told West that his niece was still in shock after finding out about her father, and that she wasn't dealing well with it. She knew it was true but didn't want to believe it, and it was eating her up. Pankake asked West's advice on how to get her some help so she could make it through this. This sort of request happens quite often in police investigations. The people involved in them will ask the officers for information or help outside the officer's scope of expertise. But West did what all good police officers do: He didn't let the person lose faith. He told Pankake that he would see what he could do to get Palma some help.

As Pankake and West talked about the case, West was properly skeptical that this could be the break that had never come in the North LaSalle Street case. He well remembered the fallout from the Carol Schultz resurrection of the case, and so he knew he needed to be cautious. However, he wasn't going to just brush it off, either. Pankake said that when Palma brought the letter to him, they had talked about it and decided that they needed to investigate the claims a bit before they did anything about it. If true, they knew these facts could do serious damage to her father's memory and the family name. However, once they finally discovered that a crime like the one Harbison described in the letter actually had occurred, even though Palma still didn't want to believe it, the two of them agreed that they needed to talk to the police about it, that their main concern was for the families of the three victims, that they deserved to know what had actually happened.

In their conversation, West learned that Jeff Pankake had also worked for Ted Uland's oil drilling company. He said that Fred Harbison had been the foreman on an oil well crew he had worked on. He said Harbison had been a tough man who had expected hard work out of his crew. Pankake also said he suspected that Harbison, along with working in the oil drilling business with Uland, also did Uland's dirty work; he thought that Harbison had been involved in a lot of other crimes for Uland. When West pointed out that Harbison had typed his name but not signed the letter, Pankake said that this was likely because Harbison was afraid that the letter might be discovered while he was still alive, and without his signature it would be hard to prove that the letter had actually come from him. Pankake said that Harbison knew how to get away with things.

"He [Harbison] supposedly did a lot of work for Uland," said West. "There was speculation that he had set fire to some property owned by Uland up in New Augusta. There was also property that was a business in Princeton or Jasper owned by Uland that was set on fire. The word was that he would do all of the dirty work for Uland."

West then asked Pankake about the yellow Road Runner that Harbison had mentioned in the letter. West knew that each piece of the letter had to be authenticated if it was to be believed. Pankake said that he remembered the car, and that he would look for some old photographs of it. Finally, West asked whether Pankake would be available if he drove down to Princeton the next week. (Princeton is the county seat for Gibson County and has a population, according to the 2010 Census, of 8,644.) Pankake said that he would clear his calendar and be available to help in any way he could.

On November 28, 2000, Deputy Deborah Borchelt had to drive to Pendleton, Indiana, to pick up two prisoners, which necessitated her passing near Indianapolis. So, upon the request of Sergeant Roy West, she stopped in at the Homicide Office on the way. West wanted to get her opinion of Angel Palma's state of mind before he went to southern Indiana to interview her. Quite often, people who want to admit to crimes or accuse others of them are suffering from serious mental problems. Borchelt said that Palma seemed stable enough, and that she might very well be telling the truth. Deputy Borchelt also brought with her the two audiotapes of her own conversations with Palma.

The following day, Sergeant West traveled to Princeton, Indiana, which sits about 150 miles southwest of Indianapolis. West drove to Jeff Pankake's house and spoke with him first. Pankake confirmed what his niece had told Deputy Borchelt, that Harbison had left school after the eighth grade and that the letter had been worded just as he would have spoken. Pankake told West that he personally felt the letter should be made public not only so that the families of the three murdered men could finally have some answers, but also so that Palma could put this behind her and move on. He said that she was still not dealing well with it. He felt that making the letter public might force her to face up to it and give her some closure.

In the interview, after talking about Palma and the letter, Pankake told Sergeant West that though he had worked for some time with both men, neither Harbison nor Uland had ever mentioned the North LaSalle Street murders in his presence. He believed he would remember it. However, he added that he felt Harbison was totally capable of doing what he said he'd done in the letter.

Harbison, according to Pankake, could at times be a very violent man, someone who liked to use fear to control people. He also mentioned that Harbison had hinted several times at being involved in other murders. Pankake added that he thought Harbison might have been picked up once by the police for kidnapping and attempted rape, but that no charges were ever brought against him. The man, he said again, knew how to get away with things.

When asked to describe Fred Harbison, Pankake told West that he had been a large man, who wore a size 18 ring. Pankake said that he had seen him knock men down with a backhand, and confirmed that Harbison always carried a six-inch bladed knife with him, and occasionally would also carry a gun. He said that Harbison loved fast, loud cars, like the yellow Road Runner he had owned in the 1970s.

Following this interview, Detective Roy West drove to Angel Palma's house to talk with her. He asked her about going to the Gibson County Sheriff's Office on November 17, and about how she had come into possession of the letter her father had written about the North LaSalle Street murders.

Palma said that she had been speaking with her stepmother and asked if there was anything left of her father's from a safety deposit box he had owned. She was looking for pictures or any other remembrances of her father, with whom she had shared a very close, loving relationship. He had died just a couple of years before and she still missed him terribly. Her stepmother told her that there was a letter her father had talked about for years, which she later gave to her. Palma said she didn't read the letter right then, but stuffed it in her coat pocket and took it home.

The envelope, she said, was old and yellowed. It was also sealed, but once she got home she opened it and read the letter. She told West that she just couldn't believe the letter's contents. This wasn't the loving father she knew. It was some kind of sick joke. It shook her up so much that she handed the letter to a friend named Ron Smith, who happened to be at her house, and asked him read it. She simply didn't want it to be true. She wanted it to be some kind of hoax or joke, and apparently she hoped Ron would confirm this. Palma told West that the envelope the letter was in was addressed to the *Indianapolis Star* newspaper, and that it was a copy and not the original letter. She could tell because the copy had been made on a machine that needed serious cleaning.

After letting Ron read the letter, and apparently not getting the response from him she wanted, which was that it wasn't true, Palma said that she asked him not to say anything about it. She then took the letter and showed it to her uncle, Jeff Pankake. She said that Jeff's eyes got real big when he saw the letter, and he told her that he wanted to scan a copy of it into his computer. Apparently, he rightly feared that if he didn't, knowing Palma's state of mind, it could become lost or be destroyed.

Palma again told West that at first she didn't believe the letter. She thought that maybe it was some kind of trick or something. This wasn't the father she knew, even though she realized that other people had seen Fred Harbison much differently than she had. Palma said that she decided to talk with the police because she wanted to see if what her father had written in the letter was even possible, and that was why she went to the Gibson County Sheriff's Office.

When asked about her father's relationship with Ted Uland, Palma recalled one time she had gone with her father to see Uland. Her father wouldn't let her go in, but instead had made her lock the doors to the truck when he got out and told her not to open them for anyone. She said that when her dad came back he was angry and told her that Uland owed him a half million dollars. He never told her what it was owed for.

West then asked her how she came into possession of the second letter, the original, which had been addressed to the chief of police in Indianapolis. Palma said that she went back to her stepmother's house to look through her father's things, again hoping perhaps to find something that would show her the letter wasn't true. She didn't. Instead, she found another sealed envelope containing the original letter folded up inside an insurance policy. Palma then repeated the story she'd told Deputy Borchelt, about how she later put both letters into her purse, but said that while she was at the hospital for observation, they'd apparently both disappeared. She couldn't imagine who had known about them or would want them. Palma promised to try to find the letters.

Knowing that all of this information would need verification, Sergeant West then asked Palma about any typewriters she or her mother had, and whether she would have any problem with him taking them for a while and having them compared with the typing on the letter. Palma said she would have no problem, that would be fine. She also told him that, yes, her father had owned a yellow Road Runner, and that she had some old pictures of it. At the end of the interview, West realized that, without the original letter, much of the investigation depended on Angel Palma's reliability. West knew he had to size her up and decide whether or not what she was telling him was the truth. He was inclined to believe her.

"From my talking with her [Angel Palma], she seemed credible in the sense of how she felt about her father and her love for him," West said. "I just didn't get the feeling she was making any of this up."

After finishing up with Palma, Sergeant West then went to talk to Palma's friend Ron Smith. He confirmed that Palma had seemed really upset and had asked him to read the letter from her father. The letter, he confirmed, had talked about Harbison killing three guys up in Indianapolis in 1971. He said that Jeff Pankake had told him that Palma's dad was kind of crazy and it was possible he'd have done things like that. Smith also recalled that the letter had said something about a yellow car.

Following this interview, Sergeant West then headed back north to Indianapolis to begin his investigation. He knew he had a lot of work to do, but he also knew that he would have to do it only in any free time he could find. As a cold case, it wasn't his top priority. At that moment, West had several much more current murder cases assigned to him, cases that he knew simply couldn't wait and would require him to often put the North La-Salle Street case aside. This case, now almost thirty years old, simply couldn't claim priority over the more recent cases. Nevertheless, he was determined to thoroughly investigate the information he had received from Palma, Pankake, and Smith. He would somehow find the time.

At this point, it was decided to let the Prosecutor's Office know about what West had found out. Just like the police department, the Prosecutor's Office had been embarrassed by the North LaSalle Street case. The prosecutor had promised in the midst of all of the huge publicity surrounding the grand jury indictments back in 1996 to prosecute the case with all of the resources of his office. Then he had been forced to call a press conference and say that he was dropping all the charges.

The day after New Year's 2001, West contacted the Marion County Prosecutor's Office and advised them of the information he had and that he intended to pursue it further. After what had happened in the Carroll Horton debacle, it was expected that the Prosecutor's Office would be skittish about wanting anything to do with the case, but it still made sense to keep them fully advised, particularly since if the information proved true, West would be asking for the case to be cleared. As expected, one of the deputy prosecutors told West that, after the Carroll Horton incident, it was unlikely that Prosecutor Newman would want anything to do with the case. Still, West scheduled a meeting with them for January 8,

2001, so that he could show them what he had uncovered so far.

The police department was also leery, with good reason, and Detective Roy West was called into a meeting with the top brass, who were worried about another blast of publicity over solving this case, only to be followed by them having to meekly say, "Never mind, we were wrong." It was their jobs on the line, too: Unlike merit ranks (such as sergeant, lieutenant, and captain, which are permanent and attained through competitive testing and interviews), appointed ranks (such as major, deputy chief, assistant chief, and chief of police) can be taken away at any time and for any reason, and there is no appeal. The deputy chief and chief of police certainly didn't want to see their ranks ripped away over a thirty-year-old murder case that had already bombed twice.

At the meeting with the chief of police, who read the letter, it was agreed that the best thing to do was not to release any information at all to the press, but to thoroughly investigate the case and have some really hard proof before anything was announced.

And so West went back to work on the case whenever he could. From everything he had heard and seen, this appeared to be the best clue the police department had ever received about the North LaSalle Street murders.

CHAPTER THIRTEEN

Sergeant Roy West realized that, before he could decide on the relevance of what he had found out from Angel Palma, he had to go get the old case file on the North LaSalle Street murders and read through every piece of it. Although he had been peripherally involved in the case in the mid-1990s and had a general knowledge of what had happened, he didn't have an in-depth understanding of it. West knew that if he was really going to be able to use Palma's new information, he needed to be intimately acquainted with every detail of the case so that he would understand how everything he had heard so far would fit into it. He had to know every fact that the detectives in 1971 had known.

But if he was going to *really* understand the case, West also knew that he had to get the evidence the detectives had collected in 1971 out of the property room and examine it firsthand. He needed to look at the paperwork the original detectives had taken from B&B Microfilming, examine any paperwork from Gierse and Hinson's time at Records Security Corporation, look at the bloody clothing and bedding material, and he especially needed to examine the coroner's exhibits.

Before doing this, though, West sent to the crime lab six knives that had belonged to Fred Harbison, which Palma had allowed him to take. She said that her father had always had plenty of knives, and, as Pankake had also stated, he had always carried at least one with him. West asked that the crime lab check the knives for traces of human blood. It had been almost thirty years since the murders, and West knew it was a long, long shot, but at least he would know he had tried. (Unfortunately, however, as expected, the crime lab would later report that they could find no traces of human blood on them.)

After sending the knives to the lab, West went to retrieve the case files. Old homicide case files are kept in the subbasement of Indianapolis police headquarters, stored in boxes stacked on floor-to-ceiling shelves. These shelves sit behind heavy gauge metal fencing and a locked door. Only homicide detectives and specially authorized personnel are allowed access to them. West took the elevator down, unlocked the door to the storage area, and after a small search found the box with case number 786420-D, the North LaSalle Street murders, written on it. West grabbed the box and then stopped one floor up at the police department property room to get the evidence in the case.

There he discovered a gut-wrenching problem, however: To West's shock, when the clerk checked the computer, West was told that there was *no* evidence. It had all been destroyed. When West had the property room clerk check the computer again, and then even manually search for the evidence, he found that indeed all of the evidence the detectives had collected in 1971, every bit of it, had been inadvertently destroyed. There was absolutely nothing left from the 1971 investigation.

Although there had been the mix-up in 1984 that had resulted in the evidence from the North LaSalle Street murders being wrongly marked to be destroyed, at least that error had been discovered in time for some of the evidence to have been found and recovered. Now, it appeared, even this rescued property had been disposed of.

West pulled up the paperwork and found that on April 28, 1999, a uniformed superior officer (not someone working homicide) had authorized the destruction of the remainder of the evidence from the North LaSalle Street murders. This evidence, according to the paperwork, had been destroyed on October 10, 2000, just over a month before Angel Palma first walked into the Gibson County Sheriff's Office.

That was impossible, West thought. Since there is no statute of limitations on murder, the police department should never get rid of evidence on open murder cases.

However, in reality, mistakes do happen. Again, as with the destruction of evidence in 1984, this wasn't part of any conspiracy of the murderer in league with the police, but simply an attempt by the property room personnel to clean out old evidence in order to make room for new evidence. At the Indianapolis Police Department, a property disposition form for evidence (on which an officer can check either "destroy" or "retain") is sent to the investigating officer of old cases every few years. But if the officer who handled the case is no longer employed by the police department, through retirement or resignation, the form is then sent to that officer's former supervisor.

This is apparently what happened in the North La-Salle Street case. The property disposition form had originally been sent in April 1999 to Lieutenant Michael Popcheff (Chief Joe McAtee and Lieutenant Jim Strode had retired years earlier). However, in April 1999, Pop-cheff had also just retired a couple of months earlier, and so they sent the form to one of his superior officers, who signed off for the evidence to be destroyed, apparently without knowing anything about the case.

Though in no way malicious, it was sloppy of this officer not to have researched the homicide casebook to check on the status of the investigation before authorizing such a thing. The officer who signed off to dispose of the North LaSalle Street evidence could have easily called the Homicide Office and had someone check the homicide casebook for him. Why he didn't bother to do so is unknown.

Immediately following his discovery that the evidence had been destroyed, West used the telephone in the property room to call the Identification Branch. He wanted to be certain they at least still had the unidentified fingerprints from North LaSalle Street (minus, of course, the one lost fingerprint that the fingerprint technician had carried around with him). Thankfully, they did, so West told them about the evidence problem and asked that they be absolutely certain to retain the fingerprints. Since there was nothing he could do about the destroyed evidence other than write a memo to the deputy chief of investigations, West left the property room and went back up to his desk on the third floor of police headquarters and began reading the homicide case file, which was hundreds of pages long.

The case file took some time to read, but to be certain he felt intimately acquainted with the investigation, West not only read the entire file, but also retyped several hundred of the most important pages of it. He felt this would help him remember critical details. After he had done this, West was confident that he knew all he could about the case. He felt certain he knew enough now to work on the new leads he had.

Along with her father's knives, Angel Palma had also given Detective West a box of Fred Harbison's personal papers. Harbison appeared to have been a very careful man, who likely wouldn't leave any incriminating papers lying around, but West also knew it was worth checking them out. He examined the papers, but, as expected, didn't find anything of value to the case. West then went back to work, again realizing how the letter from Fred Harbison would be much more persuasive if he had the original rather than just the fax of a scan.

Fortunately, on December 5, 2000, Palma located

the original letter and the copy that she had gone to the Gibson County Sheriff's Office about, though she didn't say where they had been or how she found them. (Some speculated that perhaps Palma had had the letters all along but had been torn emotionally between exposing her father as a cold-blooded killer and showing compassion for the families of the victims.)

On December 11, 2000, West met a Captain Bottoms from the Gibson County Sheriff's Office at the Indiana Law Enforcement Academy in Plainfield, Indiana, just west of Indianapolis, and took possession of the original letter and copy. When West examined them, he found that they matched exactly the scanned/faxed version Jeff Pankake had sent him, and that they indeed looked years old. Suddenly, a case that had been very questionable at first now appeared much more solid.

"I was skeptical about the letter at first," admitted West. "But once I saw the envelopes they had been in, which were old and yellowed, and once I read the letter and spoke with Angel Palma I felt comfortable that there really was something to this." While the letters alone weren't enough, they were more of a break than the case had ever had before. For the first time, it seemed possible that the police would be able to finally solve this case. But West had much more confirmation to do before the case could be designated as closed.

Coincidentally, around the same time West received the original typed letter and photocopy and was ready to begin his investigation in earnest, the police received a tip through Crime Stoppers that an anonymous caller had named a suspect never heard of before in the North LaSalle Street murders. The suspect had apparently told a female friend of his that he had been the one who had killed the three guys on North LaSalle Street. The woman told Crime Stoppers that she didn't know if his story was true or not, that maybe he'd just been trying to impress or scare her, but she said she knew he was perfectly capable of doing such a thing. She said she had called Crime Stoppers because she knew she could do it anonymously, and feared what the man would do if he found out that she was the one who had reported him.

Based on the man's arrest record, it certainly appeared that he had the background for it. In the early 1970s a judge had sentenced him to fifteen to twenty-five years in prison for beating a child to death. The man also had a number of firearms convictions on his record. However, with just a little questioning and investigation, he was easily dropped as a suspect. He didn't know any of the things he should have. He was just trying to impress someone.

Because that sort of bragging had happened so often in the thirty years since the murders, West hadn't been disturbed by it, but had kept on with his investigation of the Harbison letter. After he had finished reading and retyping the case file on the North LaSalle Street murders, West found a number of factors in the case that led him to believe that Ted Uland had certainly been a viable suspect. Two of the victims had stolen equipment and money from him, and they were also putting him out of business by taking his best customers. But most important, Uland had collected $150,000 from New York Life Insurance Company after their deaths.

The original detectives had listed Uland as a suspect right away but couldn't get past his alibi. He had called Gierse and Hinson from southern Indiana at 9:00 and 9:30 P.M. on the night of the murders. That had been checked out thoroughly by the detectives. He had also been seen that night in southern Indiana by reliable witnesses. In 1971, it would have been a three-hour drive each way. The original detectives had thought it possible that Uland might have hired someone to do it, but no one had had any idea whom. Uland was known to have a lot of rough people working for him, but no one had a record indicating anything like this. (Fred Harbison, as West would later find, had a clean police record.)

West also found through his research that although Uland had been scheduled to take a lie detector test about the murders and had shown up for it several times, various circumstances (such as he and his lawyer spending hours going over stipulations for the test) had prevented him from ever actually going through with it. Consequently, Uland stayed a viable suspect for a long time. Still, in 1971, Uland had been just one of several dozen possible suspects. The three victims had made so many enemies that the list of suspects had simply kept growing, and in 1971 some of these other suspects had also looked very viable.

West's next move, after finishing the case file, and

before working on the new information about the North
LaSalle Street murders, was to contact the FBI and ask
them to research whether Ted Uland and Fred Harbison
had ever been fingerprinted, so that he could compare
their fingerprints with the unidentified fingerprints from
North LaSalle Street. The FBI keeps a huge database of
fingerprints (which is also connected to their national
AFIS system), some of these fingerprints having been
taken by federal law enforcement agencies, some of them
sent to the FBI by local police departments, and many of
them coming from individuals fingerprinted for other
reasons, such as a security check or enlisting in the military. As it turned out, Harbison had never had his fingerprints sent to the FBI for any reason, but Uland's were
on file due to his time in the military. The FBI forwarded
a copy of his fingerprints from the army to West. Uland's
fingerprints, however, didn't match any of the unidentified fingerprints found on North LaSalle Street. (Of
course, even if they had, this wouldn't have proven anything since Uland had been at the North LaSalle Street
house several times, and even had a key for it.) What West
had really needed were Harbison's fingerprints. His fingerprints at the North LaSalle Street house would have
likely closed the case.

West also obtained, as a part of his investigation, the
death certificates for both Uland and Harbison. Ted
Uland had died first, on February 20, 1992, of metastatic
lung cancer. Fred Harbison died on January 21, 1998, of
an acute myocardial infarction (heart attack). These documents had to be obtained because criminal cases can be

cleared in several ways. They can be cleared by the arrest of a suspect, and they can also be exceptionally cleared when the police know who committed a crime, but for some reason, such as the death of the suspect, an arrest cannot be made.

As he continued his investigation, West realized that if he was going to be able to confirm the contents of Fred Harbison's letter, he needed to return to southern Indiana and talk to some more people who might be able to verify what it said. On January 9, 2001, West made the long drive again to the Princeton area. The first person he talked to there was Joyce Harbison, Fred Harbison's widow.

Widows, like ex-wives, can be great sources of information about their former husbands if their marriages weren't happy. The best way, West knew, to find out how Joyce Harbison felt about her husband was to simply come out and tell her what he was suspected of.

"She wasn't stunned," West recalled after telling Joyce Harbison what he was investigating. "Actually, she thought he was capable of doing such a thing, based on what he had done for Uland over the years. She had no knowledge that he did it, but she made the statement that she wouldn't be surprised if he was involved in it."

As they talked, Joyce told West that her husband had worked a number of years for Ted Uland at his oil drilling company. She didn't have a very high opinion of Uland. She said that he was sneaky and always trying to rip someone off. In addition, she said that Uland consistently seemed to be in debt, and that he was constantly being sued by someone. The man couldn't be trusted, she felt.

When asked about any weapons her husband might have had or carried, Joyce told West that Fred had always carried knives, and that he liked to keep them razor-sharp. He would sit in front of the television and sharpen them. She also said that he carried a pistol, but that he had a permit to do so. Along with this, she added something very important: She said that her husband always kept a heavy metal pry bar in all of the vehicles he drove. West made a particular note of this, since all three of the men on North LaSalle Street had been struck in the head multiple times with a long metal object.

Moving on in the interview, West needed to know about the letters. He needed to be as certain as possible that the letters he had been given by Palma had really been written by Fred Harbison.

"I asked her [Joyce Harbison] about [the contents] and she said the letters were never opened," said West. "She didn't know what was in them."

Joyce told West that her husband had claimed that Uland owed him a lot of money for a poker debt. She said her husband had instructed her that if by the time he died he hadn't been paid she was to send the letters off. Joyce told West that Fred had talked about the letters a number of times over the years, and that she had seen the sealed envelopes several times before her husband died. Harbison had finally put them in his lockbox at the bank, however, and she forgot about them. When she emptied his lockbox after he died, she found the letters and brought them home with the rest of the contents. However, she soon forgot about them again. After all, her husband had died and so had Uland. It was just a poker debt, so to her the letters seemed valueless and simply sat in the house for several years with the rest of her husband's property.

"Joyce said that the letters had been in the house for a long period of time," West said. "After Angel Palma's father died, Angel asked for any personal items of her father's that her stepmother had. Joyce turned over one letter to Angel, and then later turned over a second that had been with his insurance policy."

When asked about the cars her husband had owned, Joyce confirmed that Fred had owned a yellow Road Runner. She also said that he'd had an extensive knowledge of knots and that he'd had to tie a lot of knots in his job in the oil fields. She commented that he liked to show off the kind of knots that got tighter if a person struggled against them. West made another special note of this. In their original investigation in 1971, the detectives had sent off to the FBI Laboratory in Washington, D.C., some knots in the cord used to tie up the victims. The detectives had asked for any information the technicians at the laboratory might have about the knots, but the FBI hadn't been able to help.

Joyce also commented that her husband had been big and strong, and that he'd liked to fight and was involved in a lot of brawls. She added that he always wore boots. West also paid extra attention to this, since in the homicide case file he had seen the photograph of a boot print that had been made in the blood. He knew the detectives had found the print in the hallway of the house on North LaSalle Street and that, in the letter, Harbison had specifically said that he had buried his boots that night after the murders.

She then told West that for a while her husband had been on disability, but that he had continued to work for Uland, and had been paid under the table. When West asked her about any illegal activities her husband might have done for Ted Uland, she said that she knew he had done some illegal things for him, but when pressed for specifics, Joyce told him that she would rather not comment. West then asked about any typewriters Joyce and her husband might have had. She said there were four, and she gave West permission to take them all with him. She also gave him two revolvers that had belonged to her husband.

West additionally obtained a bill of sale from Joyce. It was for a Mayhew Model 1000 Drilling Rig, mounted on the back of a GMC truck. Uland had sold it to Harbison for $10, practically for free. West wondered if it could have been part of a payoff for illegal activities. Also, Joyce Harbison told West that Uland had paid her husband a salary of $200 per week, whether he worked or not, and in addition had always supplied him with a truck. This would have been a nice sum in the 1960s and '70s. It certainly seemed to West that Uland and Harbison had had a relationship in which Uland had wanted to keep Harbison as happy as he could.

After finishing his interview with Joyce Harbison,

West drove over and talked with Jeff Pankake again. He wanted, if possible, to find the typewriter the letter from Fred Harbison had been written on. If he could find it in a place where Harbison lived or visited regularly, then this would add tremendously to the letter's authenticity. Pankake said he didn't think that Palma's mother had any typewriters in her house, but that she had had one in the office of her ceramics business. However, he added, a fire at the business had melted it. Pankake then gave West the names of some other people who had also known Fred Harbison and who might be able to give him some more information.

When West returned to Indianapolis, he sent the four typewriters from the Harbison house to the crime lab, requesting that they be checked against the typeface on the letter. He also sent along the two revolvers Joyce Harbison had said belonged to her husband. West asked the crime lab to check the revolvers for any traces of blood. Again, a long shot like the knives, since it had been thirty years since the murders, but still, West knew he had to try. (But the revolvers, like the knives earlier, ultimately tested negative for blood.)

Later, the crime lab would report that although one of the four typewriters definitely *hadn't* been used to type the letter, they were unable to test the other three because they were very old and the technicians couldn't find any ribbon for them. While not the ironclad proof West had wanted, this at least still fit the story that Harbison had typed the letter a long time ago. West eventually returned the typewriters and revolvers to Joyce.

* * *

Detective Sergeant Roy West, as a part of his investigation, also had the National White Collar Crime Center in Richmond, Virginia, conduct research on Ted Uland. The Center found that during his life Uland had constantly had tax liens filed against him, and that he was also regularly sued. The result of this research showed that Ted Uland consistently had money problems, and that in 1971 he needed that $150,000 very badly. The motive for murder was certainly there. And while $150,000 is a large sum today, in 1971 it would have been huge.

Following this, the investigation next took West to Bloomington, Indiana, about fifty miles southwest of Indianapolis, where he had made an appointment to talk with Edward Dean Watson, the insurance agent who had written the $150,000 key man life insurance policies on Bob Gierse and Bob Hinson thirty years earlier. West said in his report that Watson had at first been reluctant to talk with him, telling West that he was concerned about a lawsuit if Uland's family was forced to return the insurance money. However, after being assured by West that he had no interest in the legitimacy of the insurance payout, but rather was only concerned about a criminal investigation, Watson agreed to talk with him.

Ed Watson told West that he and Ted Uland had been very close—they had been fraternity brothers at Indiana University, Uland had been best man at Watson's wedding, and for a time Uland had even dated Watson's sister. Naturally, this made West cautious. He knew that anything Watson said about Uland would be couched in this context of good friends. Watson said that after he went to work for New York Life Insurance Company he wrote a number of policies for Uland and his family. He stated that he had been the one who had recommended to Uland that he get the key man policies on Gierse and Hinson.

He remembered Uland telling him about his new business venture into microfilming and microfilm storage, and that he seemed very excited about it, and very enthusiastic about the future of the business. Uland saw it growing tremendously in the coming decade. It was, he said, the answer to the records storage problem for businesses. Watson also told West that he had once visited Records Security Corporation in Indianapolis while writing the key man policies, and that he wasn't impressed at all with the business. He said that everyone seemed to be just sitting around. For all of the promise Uland had seen in the business, Watson didn't think his employees shared the same vision.

Of Uland's financial condition, Watson said that one day he would have money and the next day he would be broke. He never put any money aside for the future. Watson told West that when he read about the murders in the newspaper, he recognized the men as the two he had written the key man life insurance policies on, and so he called the home office of New York Life to see if the policies were still in effect. He found that they were in their grace period. Watson said he then called Uland and told him about what he had read in the paper and also that he had checked and found that the policies were still in effect. Watson had expected some sort of reaction, but he said that Uland didn't seem very upset at all about the murders, even though he also claimed to Watson that this was the first he had heard of the incident.

Watson then told West about how his company had delayed paying the claim because the police in Indianapolis had said that Uland was a suspect in the murders. They couldn't pay off until the police no longer listed him as a suspect. Uland, though, Watson went on, while never seeming very upset about his former employees having been murdered, had called him over and over for months checking on the insurance claim, asking when it would be paid. But Watson said he couldn't do anything as long as the police still considered Uland a suspect. He said he got the impression that Uland was under serious financial pressure at the time and needed the money very badly.

West realized that this was a very different Uland from the one who had told the meeting in the Prosecutor's Office that Gierse and Hinson had been like family to him, and who'd said that he hoped the insurance wouldn't pay off because it would make him look bad.

Watson told West that he and Uland had discussed the case a number of times, with Uland proposing several theories about what had happened. Uland told Watson that Gierse and Hinson had been involved in buying stolen goods from a burglary ring, and that might have been what got them killed. Also, Uland offered the theory that the men might have messed around with the wrong man's girlfriend or wife. That could certainly have gotten them killed.

Watson then said that Uland told him the police in Indianapolis had wanted him to take a lie detector test, but since the police wanted to do it themselves and his lawyer had insisted it be conducted by an independent operator, as far as Watson knew Uland had never ended up taking the test. Watson also told West that eventually he received a telephone call from Lieutenant Joe McAtee, telling him that Uland was no longer a suspect in the murders. Once the police department had dropped Uland as a suspect, Watson said, his company finally paid the claim in December of 1972, and he delivered the check personally to Uland.

As West was wrapping up the interview, he said in his notes that Ed Watson expressed concern about how this investigation would impact the Uland family if it was discovered that Ted Uland had been involved. It certainly wouldn't be a good legacy for Ted Uland, Watson said. West replied that he had a responsibility to the families of the victims to find out the truth about what had happened. His job was simply to investigate the case, and he couldn't worry about how the outcome affected someone's legacy.

By this point, Detective Roy West felt that he now had a pretty good idea of what had happened in the North LaSalle Street murders, but he had to be absolutely certain. So on March 28, 2001, he returned to talk again with Joyce Harbison. West wanted to be positive that the letters he had in his possession were the letters she had given to Palma. He needed to be assured that these were the letters she had seen years before, the ones that her husband had given her instructions about. Joyce verified that they were. She also said again that she thought it was possible her husband might have committed the murders because of the kind of things he would do for Ted Uland back then. He had done a lot of Uland's dirty work, she said. She also told West that her husband had talked a long time ago about burying his boots one night in a groundhog hole. She didn't know why, and probably hadn't wanted to. West left Joyce Harbison's house feeling that he no longer had any doubt of Uland and Harbison's involvement.

"Well, there's been so many different theories about how it happened and who was involved," said West. "I think that logically this is the only theory that makes sense. When you look at the business angle of the crime, the whole motive lies within that aspect. I know there's theories about the men's game of dating all of these women and such, and theories about organized crime being involved. None of it fits. This does."

On the same day he spoke to Joyce Harbison, West also spoke again with Angel Palma. Palma had contacted him with information about a possible accomplice, George Smith,[1] who might have assisted her father in

---

[1] Denotes pseudonym

the North LaSalle Street murders. She told West that she hadn't said anything about it before because Smith still lived nearby and she was worried about the safety of her family. But now that she had given him the letters, she felt she had to tell him everything.

Palma said that Smith had worked with her father and had also been friends with him. She said she suspected that he might have helped Fred Harbison on North La-Salle Street because her father would do things for Smith that he would never do for anyone else; Harbison would go out of his way to accommodate this man. Whatever Smith wanted, he got. Palma told West that she knew it was dangerous to give him this information, but she felt it was important that he know about it.

"Angel [Palma] was fearful of saying anything because the man lived in the next town, and he knew all of her family members," said West. "She was afraid if she said anything he would hurt her or her family because he would know where the information came from."

On April 8, 2001, West talked with George Smith, who confirmed that he had lived in the Jasper, Indiana, area in 1971, and that he had worked with both Fred Harbison and Ted Uland. Smith said he had worked first with Harbison digging water wells, but then Rural Water arrived in the county and pretty much put them out of business. He described Harbison as having been a big, strong man who could be very intimidating if he wanted to be. He said that Harbison could be in your face screaming at you one minute, and then patting you on the back the next. It was very unsettling, because a person never knew which way it would go. When asked about the cars Harbison had driven, the man recalled the yellow Road Runner. He added that Harbison often carried a .38 caliber revolver, and always had a knife that he kept extremely sharp.

After Fred Harbison's water well business went under, Smith said that he started working for Ted Uland in his oil well business, and that he was working for Uland at the time of the North LaSalle Street murders. When asked about Uland, Smith didn't offer a very high opinion of him. He said that Uland had had a reputation for trying to skip out on paying bills and for screwing people over every chance he got. No one, he said, would take Ted Uland's checks. He also told West that the guys he worked with at the oil well business used to tease Uland that they were all going to get big bonuses when the insurance money from Gierse and Hinson came in. Uland never responded, he said, but would just shrug it off. Smith also told West that he had always thought Uland had something to do with the North LaSalle Street murders. He said he had no proof, just his belief.

Finally, West got to the reason he had come. He asked the man about his own involvement in the North LaSalle Street murders. George Smith denied any knowledge of them. However, West wrote in his notes that he looked directly at Smith when he asked him about being involved in the murders, and that Smith paused and looked up to his left before answering. (For those detectives who have attended the Kinesic Interview and Interrogation School, this is a sign of deception.) The man also told

West that he had been to Indianapolis before, but never with Harbison or Uland, and never to the North LaSalle Street address.

Was George Smith involved in the North LaSalle Street murders or did he have some knowledge about them? Possibly. But there's no real proof to connect him with the murders; just Angel Palma's suspicion and Detective West's belief that he was lying. However, at the end of the interview, West asked Smith if he would be willing to take a lie detector test. Smith shook his head and said no, under no circumstances would he take one. West wrote in his notes that it was likely Smith knew about how Uland never took a lie detector test and about how everything against him was ultimately dropped. Still, since the man did have a police record, West was able to obtain a copy of Smith's fingerprints, and had them compared to the unidentified fingerprints from North LaSalle Street. The Identification Branch found no match.

Once back in Indianapolis, Detective Roy West began to gather all of the notes he had taken, and all of the transcripts of the interviews he had conducted. It was time to put them together into a report to send to the Prosecutor's Office.

CHAPTER FOURTEEN

Detective Sergeant Roy West sat at his desk in the Homicide Office in the early months of 2003. Although he'd had to work on many intervening murder cases in the little over two years since he had received the first call from Deputy Borchelt, he had finally finished with the North LaSalle Street case. After combining all of the evidence he had recovered and all of the interviews he had conducted, West felt that he had enough information to request that the case be exceptionally cleared.

To this end, he had sent to the Prosecutor's Office all of the information he had gained from his investigation and interviews. West had also prepared a forty-two-page report in which he explained his reasons for deeming the evidence convincing enough to show that Fred Harbison had been hired by Ted Uland to commit the murders on North LaSalle Street. This evidence included the following:

- Fred Harbison would have no reason, other than the fact he had been cheated out of his money, to write the letter if it wasn't to be mailed until after he died. This certainly wouldn't have been a great legacy for him. And he obviously wasn't looking to falsely boast about it, as he never told his wife what he had done, let alone what was in the letter. Harbison took a tremendous risk writing this letter—though he had not signed his name to the letter, he *had* typed it, and if the letter had become known to the police before he died he would have come under strong suspicion. Clearly the police hadn't suspected him. He had gotten away with murder. But exposure of this letter would have seriously jeopardized that. Therefore, the only logical reason for writing the letter was what it appeared: He had been cheated out of his money, and this was the only way he'd apparently felt he could get back at Ted Uland.

- The letters from Harbison and the envelopes they had been in were aged and yellow, not something that had been recently produced. Also, the ink was faded—which, even if old paper and envelopes were used, an amateur forger likely wouldn't have been able to duplicate. Additionally, Harbison's widow had confirmed that she had seen the sealed envelopes years before and that her husband had talked about the letters a number of times. Joyce Harbison had also confirmed to West that the envelopes her stepdaughter had given West were the same ones she herself had given to Angel Palma, and that they were the same ones she had gotten out of the lockbox and brought home. West could see no reason for Joyce Harbison to want to lie about it. She wasn't going to profit by the exposure of her husband as a murderer. If anything it would be shameful and embarrassing.

- Fred Harbison's daughter, Angel Palma, had been the one to initiate the new direction in the North LaSalle Street case. As far as West could see, she had nothing to gain by making the letter public. Joyce Harbison and others told West that father and daughter had had a very close, special relationship, and that when Palma found the letter she had been looking for remembrances of her father. She had been in the process of looking for *good* memories; this letter certainly wasn't what she'd been seeking. And so, revealing publicly that her father had been a cold-blooded killer must certainly have caused her pain. To believe that she would make up something like this about a man she loved dearly just didn't ring true. Also, Jeff Pankake and others said that Palma, after finding the letters, had had a very difficult time dealing emotionally with it. Pankake had said that the disturbance in which Palma had ended up breaking out several of his car windows had been over her trying to cope with what the letter said. Also, there was the suspicion that no one had really taken the letters from Palma's purse while she was at the hospital, but that she had had them the whole time. She had likely simply been wrestling with the dilemma of what to do, perhaps wishing she had never said anything about them in the first place.

• Fred Harbison had known about the bloody boot print left in the house on North LaSalle Street, and wrote in the letter that he had buried his boots afterward to keep them from being identified. Joyce Harbison had also confirmed that her husband had told her many years ago about burying his boots one night in a groundhog hole.

• During the original investigation in 1971, the detectives received information that a car had been stolen from Scott Graphics just before the killings on North LaSalle Street. Scott Graphics had sold microfilm supplies to both B&B Microfilming and Records Security Corporation. This meant that Ted Uland would have been acquainted with this company. The police found the car a couple of miles south of the North LaSalle Street house the day after the murders. But more important, they found blood in the backseat. The blood was type O. All three victims on North LaSalle Street had type A blood. Fred Harbison, West discovered, had type O blood. Had that car been used as a backup transport? Had Harbison realized he would likely get bloody during the murders and didn't want to get any of the victim's blood in his own car, so he had planned to ride in this one until he got cleaned up? Possibly. Of course, the blood in the car wasn't from the victims since none of them were type O, but it could very easily have been Harbison's. The police often find that when an assailant uses a knife or some other sharp object to assault someone with, the more violent the assault and the more the victim struggles, the more likely it is that the assailant will cut himself. The North LaSalle Street murders had been particularly violent, and evidence showed that the victims had struggled against their assailant. Also, the stolen car was found south of the North LaSalle Street house, which is the direction Harbison would have been going to return home. It could all be just a coincidence, but it seems a little pat.

• A light-colored car with a 26A prefix license plate had been seen by a witness at the murder scene on the night of the crime. This prefix meant that the car came from Gibson County in southern Indiana. Fred Harbison lived in Gibson County and owned a yellow Road Runner, which would have had a 26 prefix license plate. This is also close to the area where Ted Uland lived. (It is still unclear why this information didn't bring more of a response from the original investigative team, at least one of whom still holds to the belief that it was the sex contest that got the men killed.) A car from southern Indiana, close to where

Ted Uland lived and worked, and seen at the crime scene, should have pushed the other suspects aside and put Uland up front and center.

• Witnesses also reported that the light-colored car at the murder scene had had three men sitting in it. Would Fred Harbison have brought along help? Very likely. The victims were all big men who had a reputation for liking to fight. Therefore, Harbison had to realize that there would be the possibility of a struggle. So, it is very likely that Harbison would have brought along help.

• Many of the people West talked to about Fred Harbison said that he was the kind of man who could have committed the North LaSalle Street murders, and that he had bragged about committing other murders. Even Harbison's wife hadn't doubted that her husband could have been involved in such a crime. She confirmed that Fred had done a lot of Uland's dirty work.

• The detectives in 1971 had found the remains of a cigar at the murder scene. None of the three victims smoked cigars, but Harbison, according to those who knew him, occasionally did. And of course, if Harbison had brought along help, any one of those men could have smoked the cigar. While DNA evidence today could make a clue like that crucial, in 1971, a cigar butt wasn't the kind of evidence the police could use to identify anyone.

- In 1971, the detectives had noticed something unusual about the knots used to tie up the three men. They even sent the knots off to the FBI Laboratory to have them analyzed. When West spoke with Harbison's widow, she told him that her husband had been able to tie special knots that he used in the oil well business. She said he used to like to show off knots that got tighter if someone struggled against them.

- In the letter, Harbison said that he was only supposed to kill two of the men, but that a third had shown up unexpectedly. This coincided with the theory the police in 1971 had developed. They believed that Jim Barker had arrived last and was killed simply because he showed up at the wrong time. The way the victims' cars had been parked in front of the house had shown the detectives that Barker hadn't come to the house with Bob Gierse and Bob Hinson, but had come from the opposite direction. The police believed that Gierse and Hinson had come home from their office on East 10th Street, Gierse first and Hinson at least several minutes later. Barker, they believed, had come sometime after this from his house on North Rural Street.

- A theory proposed often in the news media in 1971 was that the killings had been the work of a jealous husband or boyfriend, or that of an enraged father. At least one of the original investigators still believes this. However, to do this, the killer would have had to somehow gain entry into a house that showed no signs of forced entry, and to gain control of three big men who liked to fight and who would have known what was in store for them if they allowed themselves to be tied up. It is extremely doubtful that they would have meekly submitted.

- Consequently, with this scenario there would have to have been a struggle, probably a violent one. However, with this kind of fight, the blows to the men's heads would have been to the front, and not the rear. Also, while this scenario would have certainly involved a fight, the house showed no signs of a struggle. The police found no broken or overturned furniture.

- Another theory proposed in 1971 was that the murders had been committed by several jealous husbands or boyfriends who had teamed up to commit the murders. This doesn't ring true because it's hard to believe that two or more amateurs would agree to commit such a brutal crime, and then never talk about it. One of them would have told a future girlfriend or wife. Also, it's hard to believe that two or more amateurs could truly have agreed to commit such a grisly crime. And again, the lack of any signs of struggle causes problems for this theory, too.

- As for the idea of a jealous husband or boyfriend enlisting the help of a professional killer, this stretches credibility considerably. How many people would know where to find a professional killer? The people who try usually end up talking to a police informant or an undercover officer. Also, if a jealous husband or boyfriend had found a professional killer, it's very likely that this killer would have eventually been caught for another crime. Murders like the North La-Salle Street killings would have been one of the first things this professional killer would want to talk to the police about and use as a bargaining tool.

• The more likely scenario is that the murderer hid in the house, sneaked up behind the victims as they came home, and then hit them in the head with a metal object, like a tire iron, knocking them unconscious. This would explain the severe lacerations to the rear and side of each man's head (Barker's so severe that it fractured his skull). This would also explain how the men ended up being bound and gagged without any signs of a struggle in the house. The fact that the men had shown some indication of attempting to struggle after being bound means that they likely came to, knew what was going to happen to them, and fought for their lives. And how did the killer get into the house in order to hide when there were no signs of forced entry? Ted Uland had a key.

• Why were the men killed so brutally? Very likely Uland wanted the crime to look like the work of a jealous husband or boyfriend. He likely wanted it to look like the work of someone enraged because another man had seduced his wife or girlfriend. The way the men were killed certainly didn't look like an insurance killing. Supporting this idea, witnesses had said that Harbison had bragged of killing a man and then cutting off his penis in order to make the murder look like the work of a jealous husband. If this was Uland's plan, it worked. Many people in 1971, including some of those in the news media, believed that, because of the brutality of the crime, it could only have been committed by someone enraged by the men. And the sex contest certainly lent support to this idea.

- Many of the people West talked to didn't have a very high opinion of Ted Uland. Almost universally, people who knew him said that Uland was not a model citizen. A number came right out and said that he was a criminal. Even Bob Gierse and Bob Hinson had expressed a certain fear of Uland after their meeting with him in Bloomington, Indiana, because they knew he would eventually find out how they were ripping him off. The two men told Ilene Combest that Uland was capable of anything if it involved money.

- Ted Uland had very conveniently telephoned the men from southern Indiana the night of the murders. This gave him an alibi that could be verified by the phone company. He also made certain to be seen in southern Indiana that night. Again, like the brutality of the crime, this seemed to push the investigation away from Uland and toward other suspects who didn't have such a good alibi. When asked about Uland calling on the night of the murders, West said, "I can see him doing that. He just distanced himself from the crime."

- According to the *Indianapolis Star*, at a court hearing in May of 1996, retired lieutenant Jim Strode said that Ted Uland had been a major suspect in 1971, even though the investigation eventually dropped him as a suspect.

- Insurance agent Edward Dean Watson told West that his old friend Uland hadn't seemed very upset at all about his former employees being murdered, but had hounded him for months about getting paid off for their life insurance policies, as he'd apparently needed the money desperately. The insurance policies had been within their grace period but soon would have become worthless. Uland had had to do something quickly or the $150,000 would have been gone.

- This is quite a different picture from the Ted Uland who told the staff in the Prosecutor's Office how close he had been to Gierse and Hinson, how much they'd respected one another, and how he'd hoped the policies wouldn't be paid off because it would make him look bad.

- Uland managed to avoid taking a lie detector test, even though he had agreed to several dates. He and his lawyer had placed so many conditions on the test that the police finally gave up. (While this in itself doesn't prove guilt, it is another element that adds to it.)

- In any murder case, the investigators must decide: Who had the best motive for the murder? In the

North LaSalle Street case, Ted Uland had an excellent motive for wanting at least two of the men dead. Actually, of all the people investigated in the case as suspects and persons of interest, Uland had the best motive. His business was going broke and he faced multiple tax liens and lawsuits. He needed cash badly. In addition, Gierse and Hinson had stolen some of his best customers, had stolen microfilm equipment from him, and had also reportedly stolen approximately $10,000 in cash from him. He had a very good reason to want to kill these men. Not only could he get revenge for the wrongs they had done him, but he could also recoup all of his losses and much more.

"There's so many things that happened with this case," West said. "But if you look right at the source at the beginning, there was Uland. And the fact that he refused to take a lie detector test tells me that there was more to it and that he was hiding something. Until you could honestly clear him out of the case there wasn't anyone else to look at as far as I'm concerned."

Detective West felt that everything Fred Harbison had said in his letter fit with what the police knew about the case. While there had been many theories about who the killer or killers had been on North LaSalle Street—from outraged boyfriends and husbands to Jimmy Hoffa and President Nixon—the scenario told by Harbison was the most logical. But most importantly, it fit all the facts of the case. With this scenario there were no unanswered questions, no bits of evidence that didn't fit.

On May 5, 2003, West received a response to his request for case clearance from Deputy Prosecutor John Commons, a man who had been involved with the North LaSalle Street case for many years. In this message Commons said, "It has long been my personal opinion that most likely Ted Uland along with unknown accomplices committed these murders . . . It is my personal recommendation, based on my years of experience and intimate knowledge of the history of this case, that it be given an exceptional clearance and closed."

The North LaSalle Street murders could finally be put to rest.

EPILOGUE

I was a police officer in the Indianapolis Police Department for thirty-eight years, retiring in February 2007 with the rank of captain. I worked for several years as Joe McAtee's administrative assistant and helped write some campaign speeches during his successful run for sheriff in 1985. Later, I served as commander of the Homicide Branch during the time of Detective Sergeant West's investigation of the North LaSalle Street murders.

The North LaSalle Street murders deeply affected many people. Friends and lovers of the three murdered men felt the loss for many years. They couldn't understand the brutality and apparent senselessness of it. But in addition to friends and lovers, the case also deeply affected the detectives who investigated it.

The victims of homicide, unlike the victims of almost all other crimes, cannot speak for themselves. And so, it is up to the homicide detectives to be their voice and to demand justice on their behalves. When this doesn't happen it disturbs the detectives greatly. All of the detectives who investigated the case in 1971 were deeply bothered that the case went unsolved for so long. But even though they were personally unable to solve it, they all moved on to have distinguished careers at the Indianapolis Police Department before continuing with other pursuits.

Joe McAtee, following the North LaSalle Street murders, was promoted to captain and then to the position of deputy chief of operations, in which he was in charge of all of the department's uniformed personnel. Following this, in January 1981, the mayor of Indianapolis appointed Joe to the job of chief of police. In 1985, he ran for election to become the sheriff of Marion County. He easily won and served as sheriff for eight years, being barred by state law from running for a third term. Today, Joe is still at the Marion County Sheriff's Office. He is a colonel and in charge of the Metropolitan Emergency Communications Agency.

After the North LaSalle Street murders, Mike Popcheff continued to work for some time as a homicide detective sergeant. Then, after Mike received a promotion to the rank of lieutenant, the police department assigned him to supervise a uniformed district on the south side of the city. Mike retired in February 1999 and presently works providing corporate security.

Jim Strode also continued to work homicides following the North LaSalle Street case, and also eventually received a promotion to the rank of lieutenant. He retired in January 1987 and ultimately ran for and won the election to be a constable in Lawrence Township of Marion County. A constable in Indiana is an officer of the court, who helps serve the court's orders. Jim, though, simply couldn't stay away from homicide investigation, and is presently back at the Indianapolis Police Department working in their cold case squad.

Roy West retired from the Indianapolis Police Department at the end of December 2007. He now works as an investigator for the Marion County Grand Jury.

Detective Sergeant Pat Stark and Captain Bob Tirmenstein have both passed away, Bob in 1997 and Pat in 2003.

Carol Schultz, following the collapse of the North LaSalle Street murder case in 1996, moved to California, where she found a job writing for a national magazine. Carol eventually returned to Indianapolis and got married. She also finally decided to do what she really loved: She became a private investigator.

There are several of Robert Gierse's, Robert Hinson's, and James Barker's relatives still alive after forty years, and in the writing of this book I attempted to contact them, but not surprisingly, received no response. Twice before, in the 1970s and 1990s, they were promised by the police that the murder of their loved ones had been or soon would be solved, and both times they were bitterly disappointed. It's very likely that they believed after the second disappointment that the case would never be solved. I hope that by the publication of this book they can finally get some closure.

ABOUT THE AUTHOR

Robert L. Snow served for thirty-eight years in the Indianapolis Police Department, retiring in 2007 with the rank of captain. While at the police department, he served in such capacities as police department executive officer, captain of detectives, and commander of the Homicide Branch. He is the author of thirteen books and has had more than one hundred articles and short stories published in magazines including *Playboy*, *Reader's Digest*, and *National Enquirer*.